What Jes

HOW TO MANAGE STRESS BIBLICALLY

By Penn Clark

2021 © Copyright by Penn Clark
Published by Wordsmith Publishing of Penn Yan, New York

What Jesus Said About Stress

How to Manage Stress Biblically

By Penn Clark

All rights reserved. This book or parts thereof may not be reproduced in any form, except for brief quotations in reviews, without the express permission of the publisher.

This material and material published on the related web pages listed herein are the creative property of Penn Clark and may not be reproduced for distribution in any form. However, they may be used for personal edification or for small group study without prior permission.

Both Discipleship House and Wordsmith Publishing are ministries of WellSpring Fellowship, which is a nonprofit 501 C3. Our office address is 217 Main St, Penn Yan, New York 14527. For current contact information and the latest editions of Wordsmith Study Guides, go to our website (www.pennclark.net).

The mission of Wordsmith Publishing is to provide teaching and training materials, using all forms of media, in order to advance the Kingdom of God both here and overseas. It is our desire to help more believers become committed disciples of the living Christ.

Scripture quotations are taken from the New King James Version®. Copyright © 1982 by Thomas Nelson, Inc. Used by permission. All rights reserved.

Scripture quotations marked (AMP) are taken from the *Amplified Bible*, Copyright © 1954, 1958, 1962, 1964, 1965, 1987 by The Lockman Foundation. Used by permission.

Scripture quotations marked (KJV) are taken from the Holy Bible, King James Version, Cambridge, 1769.

Scripture quotations marked (ESV) are taken from The Holy Bible, English Standard Version, copyright © 2001 by Crossway, a publishing ministry of Good News Publishers. Used by permission. All rights reserved.

Scripture quotations marked (MSG) are taken from THE MESSAGE, copyright © 1993, 2002, 2018 by Eugene H. Peterson. Used by permission of NavPress, represented by Tyndale House Publishers. All rights reserved.

Scripture quotations marked (NIV) are taken from the Holy Bible, New International Version®, NIV®. Copyright ©1973, 1978, 1984, 2011 by Biblica, Inc.TM Used by permission of Zondervan. All rights reserved worldwide. www.zondervan.com The "NIV" and "New International Version" are trademarks registered in the United States Patent and Trademark Office by Biblica, Inc.

Scripture quotations marked (TLB) are taken from *The Living Bible* copyright © 1971. Used by permission of

Tyndale House Publishers, Inc., Carol Stream, Illinois 60188. All rights reserved.

Scripture quotations marked (JBP) are taken from The New Testament in Modern English, copyright © 1958, 1959, 1960 J.B. Phillips and 1947, 1952, 1955, 1957 The Macmillan Company, New York. Used by permission. All rights reserved.

Scripture quotations marked (GWT) are taken from GOD'S WORD®, © 1995 God's Word to the Nations. Used by permission of Baker Publishing Group.

Edited by Edie Mourey (www.furrowpress.com).

Special thanks for their help with this project go to Heather Clark, Rebecca Levin, Hannah Wigden, Norman D. Morrison, and Marta Marino.

Photos of author by Wanda Thompson of Belleville, Ontario.

The cover photo was provided by Bigstock.com, listed as stock photo 6040223, copyright: kto

Ask us about a special rate when you order our books in bulk.

ISBN: 978-1-947472-87-7 (eBook)

ISBN: 978-1-947472-42-6 (Print)

CONTENTS

Introduction	1
What Jesus Said About Tribulation	4
Symptoms of Stress	17
Suppressed Emotions	25
Sources of Stress	33
The Wisdom of the Lord's Prayer	44
One-Day Thinking	52
Taking Charge of "What If"	58
James Under Pressure	66
Gaining a Heavenly Perspective	79
Ways to Decompress	87
A Negativity Fast	96
Learning to Breathe	106
My Book List	109
Lower Back Excises	111

ABOUT PENN CLARK

God has given Penn a unique ability to communicate His grace in a way that is both profound and practical. From the very beginning, Penn has been a diligent steward of the revelations he has been given, writing them out, polishing them, and making them available to others. Now, with more than thirty books available from a lifetime of study, each book is an example of how to handle the Word of God with integrity. Through the years, the Lord has motivated Penn to present discipleship in a way that is both inspiring and accessible, creating unique places for this to take place within the local church. The Clarks are based in the beautiful Finger Lakes region of New York, where they serve WellSpring Fellowship. To learn more about Penn, go to www.pennclark.net or www.pennclark.study

CHAPTER ONE

Introduction

One time, I met someone for lunch who had been under a lot of stress. When they finished explaining what they were going through, I reached across the table and took a handful of napkins and began writing down the names of each area of pressure they were under. Soon the table was covered with napkins, all laid out in front of them. For the first time, they could see all that they had been carrying. It also helped them recognize the sources of the pressure that had become so unmanageable.

I explained how most people would usually only be dealing with one or two sources of pressure at a time, but they had been struggling with too many at once. No wonder they couldn't sleep and were struggling with their health. It was a revelation for them to see it all laid out like that. We talked through each one, agreeing on how to approach the ones that could be resolved right away. As we did this, I began to eliminate one napkin at a time. Finally, only a few napkins were left, and these represented the most difficult sources of pressure for which there was no easy solutions. We agreed to begin trusting the Lord for His help with the pressures, putting them in His big hand in prayer right there in the restaurant. All of a sudden, their life looked more manageable. They breathed a sigh of relief and left the meeting lighter.

I won't take any time in this study to try to convince you that we are living in stressful times. There are many sources of stress; everything that is going on in our society, our government, and in these crazy Covid days. The effects of stress are manifested in so many ways—broken marriages, substance abuse, outbursts of anger, and hellish health.

I am not advocating that we live stress-free lives; I don't think that's a reasonable goal. I certainly don't live that way. I think we should reduce the amount of stress in our lives so that it is more manageable, before it hurts our health and relationships and ruins our spiritual lives.

While these are certainly stress-filled days, the apostle Paul warned the church of his day that this is nothing compared to what is coming:

But understand this, that in the last days will come (set in) perilous times of great stress and trouble [hard to deal with and hard to bear]. (2 Timothy 3:1, AMP)

One time, when Jeremiah was under a lot of stress, he complained to the Lord about the pressure and resistance he was having as a young prophet. In response, the Lord asked him,

If you have run with the footmen, and they have wearied you, then how can you contend with horses? And if in the land of peace, in which you trusted, they wearied you, then how will you do in the floodplain of the Jordan? (Jeremiah 12:5)

In other words, if you cannot manage now, how are you going to manage when things really get tough? This is one of the big takeaways during the days of lockdowns and quarantines during Covid. How well have we managed it? If we cannot survive this in our warm comfortable houses—having more food than what is good for us to eat, and entertainment and many diversions to help pass the time—how will we hold up under great tribulation?

Let's begin by laying out all the napkins to help identify the areas that are creating stress in our lives. Let's invite the Lord to teach us how to manage it better, allowing Him to take us places by the Holy Spirit where we would otherwise never go.

With every blessing, Penn

CHAPTER TWO

What Jesus Said About Tribulation

Jesus often talked about stress and the sources of it, either directly or indirectly, giving us clues as to what causes it and how to deal with it. While the word *stress* is not found in the King James Version of the Bible, it is implied in words like *tribulation* and *troubled*. Let's explore these words and others to see what they reveal to us about managing stress.

In John 16:33, Jesus stated matter-of-factly that we will have tribulation in the world:

*These things I have spoken to you, that in Me you may have peace. In the world you will have **tribulation**; but be of good cheer, I have overcome the world.*

Know that tribulation and the pressure it brings are a fact of life. Embracing them as such can actually help reduce stress. Otherwise, why would He share this with us?

From this we can see how there has always been and will always be stress in this world, but Jesus offered His peace as an alternative. In John 14:27, we see how this choice is ours:

*"Peace I leave with you, My peace I give to you; not as the world gives do I give to you. Let not your heart be **troubled**, neither let it be afraid."*

Think about that: Jesus was offering His peace, instead of circumstantial peace, which occurs when there are no problems or conflicts and everything is going smoothly. Instead, Jesus offers us His peace, which He had when the hometown crowd turned against Him and was trying to throw Him over a cliff. He offers us the peace He had when He was being confronted by angry Pharisees and when the demoniac man ran toward Him. His peace is not based on having perfect circumstances but is a peace that is present during troubled times. That's the kind of peace I need!

According to the *Strong's Concordance*, the word *tribulation* is made up mostly of *pressure* which is another word for *stress*:

TRIBULATION GK. 2347 *thlipsis*; from 2346; pressure (literally or figuratively):— afflicted(-tion), anguish, burdened, persecution, tribulation, trouble.

Jesus believed life is only going to become more stressful for both the world and the Church as things wrap up here:

*"For then there will be **great tribulation**, such as has not been since the beginning of the world until this time, no, nor ever shall be. And unless those days were shortened, no flesh would be saved; but for the*

elect's sake those days will be shortened." (Matthew 24:21–22)

One of the reasons we need to learn to deal with tribulation is because it can prevent spiritual growth, as Jesus pointed out in the parable of the sower:

*These likewise are the ones sown on stony ground who, when they hear the word, immediately receive it with gladness; and they have no root in themselves, and so endure only for a time. Afterward, when **tribulation** or persecution arises for the word's sake, immediately they stumble.* (Mark 4:16–17)

Let's read the next section of the parable, this time from *The Message*:

"The seed cast in the weeds represents the ones who hear the kingdom news but are overwhelmed with worries about all the things they have to do and all the things they want to get. The stress strangles what they heard, and nothing comes of it." (Mark 4:18–19)

What if it is not possible to live a stressed-out life and be a strong, growing Christian at the same time? Sooner or later, something must give. I think this is also the reason why some of our churches won't grow. Rather than being a place that relieves stress, our churches are often the sources of it.

NEEDING SPACE

Jesus often felt pressed upon by the crowds. He even took precautions against the press, knowing how the people would try to get close to Him:

*So He told His disciples that a small boat should be kept ready for Him because of the multitude, lest they should **crush** Him.* (Mark 3:9)

The Greek word for *crush* used here describes an ancient way that they made wine, by treading the grapes underfoot.

This is a clear picture of stress or pressure that all of us some- times feel—as if the life is being squeezed out of us:

CRUSH GK 2346. *thlib_*; akin to the base of 5147; to crowd (literally or figuratively):— afflict, narrow, throng, suffer tribulation, trouble.

Another word in the Bible that describes stress is the word *troubled*. Here it is from the *Strong's Concordance*:

TROUBLED GK. 5182 *tyrbaz_*; from *turb_* (Latin *turba*, a crowd; akin to 2351); to make "turbid," i.e. disturb:— trouble.

The word *troubled* comes from the word *crowd* or the old Roman word (Latin) *turba*.

I find it interesting that, when we are under stress, it feels like things are too crowded. People often say they need space to think or clear their heads. Perhaps this feeling of being crowded is an indication of too much stress in our lives. Getting alone, going for a walk, or decluttering our lives and schedules can make us feel better, even if our circumstances haven't changed that much. We just need some space.

To make something *turbid*, according to the *Oxford Dictionary*, means to make it cloudy or opaque. It conveys the idea of being confused. Daniel Levitin, a neuroscientist, once gave a TED talk about how the brain performs under stress. He said it releases *cortisol* which raises our heart rates, modulates adrenaline levels, and clouds our thinking.[1]

Stress *disturbs* our thinking or makes it cloudy.

We have all had those moments under stress when our minds go blank. Today, we might call it a *brain freeze*, but it is simply cortisol being released into our systems. These days, I hear people complaining about how their memory is not what it used to be, getting worse with age, but I have found that, when I have reduced the amount of stress in my life, my memory gets better. What if it has nothing to do with age? What if our body's releasing cortisol into our systems acts like a breaker so our "electrical systems" don't have a total blowout? What if blowing our breakers should act as a sign that we need some space?

When we are feeling overcrowded, we should do what Jesus did—He often slipped away from the crowds. He headed for the hills, got alone in nature, went out into the wilderness. Perhaps that is why He was found walking on water from time-to-time. What if this was the only way He could really get alone to pray and think?

JESUS EXPERIENCED STRESS

Everyone experiences stress, including Jesus, yet I cannot imagine Him walking around, wringing His shaking hands, being all "stressed-out," and not knowing what to do. Only in the old movie versions of Him do we see Him portrayed as a joyless person, haggard and nerve-strained, easily angered, and exasperated. This is one reason why I don't like most movies about Jesus. This is not how I imagine Him, but still we are told in Scripture that He experienced lots of stress. He was often pulled in different directions, both by needs and nettling. Here is an example of Jesus experiencing stress:

*Therefore, when Jesus saw her weeping, and the Jews who came with her weeping, He groaned in the spirit and was **troubled**. And He said, "Where have you laid him?"* (John 11:33–34)

The definition of the word *troubled* in this verse has to do with being agitated, as we can see in *Strong's Concordance*:

TROUBLED GK. 5015 *tarass_*; of uncertain affinity; to stir or agitate (roil water):— trouble. To agitate, trouble (a thing, by the movement of its parts to and fro) to cause one inward commotion, take away his calmness of mind, disturb his equanimity to disquiet, make restless to stir up to trouble.

This was not the only time Jesus was troubled within. As He began to talk about going to the cross, Jesus became troubled within, not for fear of dying, but because of the spiritual pressure that He was under:

*"Now My soul is **troubled**, and what shall I say? 'Father, save Me from this hour'? But for this purpose I came to this hour. Father, glorify Your name." Then a voice came from heaven, saying, "I have both glorified it and will glorify it again."* (John 12:27–28)

Then as He got alone in the forest of Gethsemane so He could pray, He came under great stress. Ironically, the word *Gethsemane* means *the place of the olive press*. It is derived from two Hebrew words: *gat*, which means *a place for pressing oil*, and *shemanim*, which means *oils.*

In biblical days, a heavy stone wheel was rolled over the olive berries, crushing them until the oil ran into a pit that could run out into clay jars. What a picture of stress!

We can also find Jesus being stressed in Mark 14:33–34, where we read:

*And He took Peter, James, and John with Him, and He began to be **troubled and deeply distressed**. Then He* *said to them, "My soul is exceedingly sorrowful, even to death. Stay here and watch."*

Perhaps the lowest point in His life was the time when He was under so much pressure that His perspiration turned to blood:

And being in anguish, he prayed more earnestly, and his sweat was like drops of blood falling to the ground. (Luke 22:44, NIV)

Jesus said that He was under so much pressure that He thought He would die right there. Matthew and Mark both noted how Jesus was *"overwhelmed with sorrow to the point of death"* (Matthew 26:38; Mark 14:34, NIV). The angels came to encourage Him again, just like they had when He was tempted in the wilderness. Somehow, they helped reduce the spiritual pressure He was under!

Having His perspiration turn to blood should also help us to see the connection between our emotional and our physical well-being. What He was feeling on the inside showed up on the outside.

PAUL EXPERIENCED STRESS

Feeling stress or being under pressure does not mean we lack spirituality or are spiritually deficient. It happened to Jesus, and it happens to us, His disciples. Chronic stress is another issue, though, and should be avoided at all costs. One of the things I respect about the apostle Paul is how free he was when describing his fears and inner struggles. His honest response to stress has often given me hope. He wrote:

*We are **hard-pressed** on every side, yet not crushed; we are perplexed, but not in despair; persecuted, but not forsaken; struck down, but not destroyed— always carrying about in the body the dying of the Lord Jesus, that the life of Jesus also may be manifested in our body.* (2 Corinthians 4:8–10)

*For indeed, when we came to Macedonia, our bodies had no rest, but we were **troubled** on every side. Outside were conflicts, inside were fears. Nevertheless God, who comforts the downcast, comforted us by the coming of Titus.* (2 Corinthians 7:5–6)

*For, in fact, we told you before when we were with you that we would suffer **tribulation**, just as it happened, and you know. For this reason, when I could no longer endure it, I sent to know your faith, lest by some means the tempter had tempted you, and our labor might be in vain.* (1 Thessalonians 3:4–5)

*Therefore, brethren, in all our affliction and **distress** we were comforted concerning you by your faith. For now we live, if you stand fast in the Lord.* (1 Thessalonians 3:7–8)

*Since it is a righteous thing with God to repay with **tribulation** those who trouble you, and to give you* *who are **troubled** rest with us when the Lord Jesus is revealed from heaven with His mighty angels. . . .* (2 Thessalonians 1:6–7)

When I read what Paul told the Thessalonians about tribulation from the *Amplified Bible*, I noticed that the authors rendered it *strain* and *stress*:

*That is the reason that, when I could bear [the suspense] no longer, I sent that I might learn [how you were standing the **strain**, and the endurance of] your faith, [for I was fearful] lest somehow the tempter had tempted you and our toil [among you should prove to] be fruitless and to no purpose.* (1 Thessalonians 3:5)

*Brethren, for this reason, in [spite of all] our **stress and crushing** difficulties we have been filled with comfort and cheer about you [because of] your faith (the leaning of your whole personality on God in complete trust and confidence).* (1 Thessalonians 3:7)

PERPLEXED

I had a sense from the Lord that we were to plant a new church in Penn Yan, but I didn't know how or where I should do it. We had no place, no people, no money, not even a name for a church, which left me feeling stuck, which rarely happens to a visionary like me. As I read my Bible one morning, I came across the verse where the apostle Paul said,

*We are hard-pressed on every side, yet not crushed; **we are perplexed**, but not in despair.* (2 Corinthians 4:8)

Two things struck me about this verse: First, I was surprised that Paul would have ever felt perplexed. You get the impression from how near he was to the Lord that he would have been beyond this. The second thing was how this word perfectly described how I felt. I took a moment to look it up in a *Strong's Greek* dictionary, and the definition for *perplexed* in this verse is, *"to have no way out, i.e. be at a loss (mentally)."*

I began by admitting aloud to myself and the Lord, "I am perplexed. I don't really know where to go or what to do, so please help me."

A couple of days later, I took a group of young men whom I had been discipling to New York City. One of the things I enjoy doing is introducing people to the Brooklyn Tabernacle's Tuesday Night Prayer Meeting. I can't describe how good this prayer meeting feels to me, and it is high on my things to do list anytime I go to the City. At the end of the meeting, Pastor Jim Cymbala invited pastors and missionaries to come forward for a time of personal ministry. I made my way down to the front and stood in line as Pastor Jim prayed for people. He came to me and laid his hands upon my head to pray. He simply stood there for a long time, not saying anything, which moved me because this was something I had been in the habit of doing myself. I felt that it allowed people to simply experience the Lord touching them, feeling beloved by Him. I could feel Jesus' hand on me. Then Pastor Jim prayed slowly, deliberately, and movingly: "Father, help this man with the perplexities of life. Lead him, guide him, helping him know what to do and how to do it."

I was deeply moved, to say the least.

Within two weeks of that prayer, God had confirmed the vision for a new church plant in Penn Yan, had given me a name for the church, and had brought key people forward who committed to help with the work, making up a core group. (Up until this time, we only had four adults and four children committed.) He gave us a building to use and a new home for Heather and me to live in. Most of this happened in one day. Then, out of the blue, Heather was called in for a job interview, where they bent over backwards to hire her. Most importantly, the Lord had given me some precious promises about what this work would become. He promised that His blessing would be upon it and that His glory would be there, which was all I really needed.[2]

To summarize, it is helpful to take time to read what Jesus said about stress. From His teaching and experience, we can safely conclude the following:

- The word *stress* is hidden in the words *tribulation* and *trouble*.

- Stress is an inevitable part of this fallen world system.

- Even the best people, like Jesus and Paul, experienced stress.

- Stress can affect our thinking, making it cloudy, causing us to become forgetful.

- God's peace is available, especially in times of tribulation.

- Chronic stress is the real issue and should be avoided.

---

1. Daniel Levitin, a neuroscientist, once gave a TED talk about how the brain performs under stress. He said it releases *cortisol* which raises our heart rates, modulates adrenaline levels, and clouds our thinking.

2. This section on being perplexed was originally printed in my book *Welcome to the Wilderness* (Penn Yan, NY: Wordsmith Publishing, 2015).

CHAPTER THREE

Symptoms of Stress

An upholsterer had been called to the office of some cardiologists to reupholster some chairs in the waiting room. As he looked at the furniture, he wondered what was wrong with the patients. The front edge of the seats and the first few inches of the armrests were completely worn out. "People don't wear out chairs this way," he told the cardiologists.

This got the doctors talking about a pattern they had noticed among many of their cardiac patients which they described as a "chronic sense of urgency." These patients often showed irritability at having to wait in line. They had difficulty relaxing and were anxious over delays. They obsessed about not wasting a moment, hurrying those around them. They spoke quickly, often interrupting, as if they were in a rush. The reason the waiting room chairs were worn out the way they were was because the patients sat on the edge of their seats, nervously rubbing at the arms of the chairs as they watched the time tick by.

The cardiologists began referring to it as "hurry sickness" as if it were a disease that came from an insatiable desire to accomplish many more things in a day than time would allow.[1]

This also helps us to see the correlation between our emotional well-being and our physical health. Jesus made this obvious when He taught about the end times. He said things would be so stressful in the last days that men's hearts would fail them from fear:

*And there will be signs in the sun, in the moon, and in the stars; and on the earth distress of nations, with perplexity, the sea and the waves roaring; men's hearts failing them from fear and the expectation of those things which are coming on the earth, for the powers of the heavens will be shaken. Then they will see the Son of Man coming in a cloud with power and great glory. Now when these things begin to happen, look up and lift up your heads, because your redemption draws near. (*Luke 21:25–28)

Stress in our bodies can manifest itself in a number of ways. Here are a few widely accepted ones that will come up in the most basic Google search:

- High blood pressure
- Stiffness or pain in your muscles, especially in your neck, shoulders, and lower back
- Having a knot in your back
- Headaches or migraines
- Digestive issues
- Clenched jaw or grinding your teeth
- Loss of sleep
- Fatigue
- Forgetfulness

Other common manifestations of stress can be seen in our habits:

- Lack of initiative
- Vegging out on movies and media
- Looking for peace in a bottle, abusing meds or alcohol
- Looking for satisfaction in excessive amounts of food or sex
- And in our emotions:
- Anxiety
- Anger
- Depression
- A sense of helplessness Tension
- Irritation Impatience

Stress itself does not produce these things, but chronic stress does. These are caused by suppressing our emotions, pushing down our fears, worries, and anger, rather than dealing with them.

LOWER BACK PAIN AND STRESS

While there are lots of physical and emotional side effects, the one I would like to take time to address has to do with lower back pain.

The first time my back went out on me, dropping me to my knees in pain, it seemed to come out of the blue. I had never experienced pain like it before. It literally took my breath away. Heather tried to help me, but I couldn't get up. Once the pain subsided, and I was able to stand upright again, the fear that it might happen again changed how I did things. I became conscious of my lower back for the first time in my life. I began to baby it, being careful not to do anything that might set it off. I concluded that I was one of those people who had a bad back.

A short time later, I happened to be attending a healing meeting when the speaker began to declare that Jesus was healing backs. I stood up because I desperately wanted to be healed. They prayed for me, and heat began to radiate down my back. I was so relieved that everything was going to be all right.

Then, sometime later, my lower back went out on me again. I cried out to the Lord, and He healed me right there during a worship service. This healing lasted awhile, but then one day while I was helping a friend move a little antique table down a narrow hallway, it went out on me again. I dropped to my knees in excruciating pain. We both began to pray for healing, but this time I felt like the Lord spoke to me, telling me that I needed to go to a chiropractor. I could barely imagine the Lord saying something like this. Back then, even doctors would not recommend that you go to a chiropractor. My friend said the Lord told him the same thing. I couldn't help but wonder, *Why won't the Lord just heal me again like He did last time?*

The chiropractor checked me out physically, and then sat me down for a serious talk. He said there was nothing wrong with my back. He told me that it was all brought on by stress. He gave me some exercises to do, which would help relax the muscles even if I were in pain and helped alleviate the problem. He explained how carrying stress was like carrying bricks around on my shoulders, compressing my lower back. If I could learn to offload whatever it was that I was carrying, the pain would go away.

That was over forty-years ago. I have not had my back go out on me since. Neither have I had to go back to a chiropractor. I have not had any operation or taken even an aspirin for back pain. I have, however, learned to read my body. I use it like a signal. Once I start feeling pain in my lower back, I know I need to begin offloading whatever stress I am carrying, and I begin doing my exercises again.

After having my own back issues, I began to notice how many pastors and professionals suffer from lower back pain.

Years later, I had discovered a book called *Healing Back Pain*, by Dr. John E. Sarno, a leading back specialist, and he confirmed everything the chiropractor had told me. Dr. Sarno found, after working with thousands of people with all kinds of pain in the back, neck, and shoulder, the pain was caused by suppressed emotions like resentment, anger, fear, and anxiety. He said that, whenever we bury these emotions rather than deal with them, we tend to breathe shallower. This prevents much needed oxygen from getting to the muscles. When our muscles become oxygen deprived, our bodies do what they were designed to do by alerting us through pain.

Dr. Sarno became so committed to this approach that he stopped doing operations altogether and began to help relieve his patients of their physical problems by addressing their emotional needs. He helped people connect the dots between what was going on in their souls and what their bodies were telling them.[2]

According to his book, one of the most difficult challenges Dr. Sarno has had is trying to get people to stop thinking they actually have "been dealt" a bad back. He says that, even if we had injured our backs, they could be healed in a couple of weeks, and we would not be stuck with the pain or injury for the rest of our lives. He said there is actually very little that can go wrong with our backs. The back is a marvel of engineering, so powerful that it is able to hold the torso upright.

We have come to believe for some reason we have "been dealt" a bad back, a mysterious physical condition, made up of degenerated disks, pinched nerves, and muscles that rupture on their own, making it difficult for us to accept the idea that these can be caused by our emotions. Believing we have "been dealt" a bad back is just too simple of a solution. It is also easier to blame the return of an old sports injury than to accept that we may have brought the pain on ourselves by the way we suppress our powerful emotions.

BRICKS ON OUR BACK

My chiropractor's counsel helped me to think of each worry or care as if it were a brick. If we had to carry one brick all day, it would affect us physically. As the bricks would begin to stack up, we would then stagger under an increasingly heavy load. No wonder our muscles ache and our lower back hurts. Physically, we are affected by the stress in our lives the same as if we are carrying actual bricks. When our bodies send messages of pain, we need to stop and offload whatever it is we are carrying. I often do this by naming each brick or care before the Lord. Sometimes, I do this over several days, depending on my load.

Because I am a very responsible person, I cannot just drop things and walk away. The deeper my sense of responsibility, the more stress, worry, and anxiety I tend to struggle with. Irresponsible people don't usually suffer much from this or bad backs.

I will often begin by picturing the Lord's big hand extended toward me, where I place the things I am responsible for into His hand. When I make the Lord responsible, I don't have to carry the weight of the cares anymore. I have learned that the Lord is very responsible and can be trusted. He cares about whatever we care about.

---

1. The section on "hurry sickness" is based upon David W. Henderson's book, *Tranquility* (Grand Rapids: Baker Books, 2015, p. 131).

2. Dr. Sarno became so committed to this approach that he stopped doing operations altogether and began to help relieve his patients of their physical problems by addressing their emotional needs. He helped people connect the dots between what is going on in their souls and what their bodies are telling them. To learn more about Dr. John E. Sarno's principles of chronic pain management, read *Healing Back Pain—The Mind-Body Connection* (New York: Warner Books, 1991).

CHAPTER FOUR

Suppressed Emotions

There was a woman who was part of a church I pastored, and she was under a lot of stress. There had been a long, drawn-out legal battle which resulted in financial stress and eventually her husband going to jail for a time. We all knew what she was going through and were concerned about her, but she waved it off. Instead of dealing with it, she simply suppressed her fears and frustrations. Then, at an outreach event where she was serving food, I happened to notice that one of her arms was limp, dangling at her side as she served people. To me, it looked as if she were having a stroke. Once we got her to the hospital to be tested, she was diagnosed as having too much stress, given medication for it, and told to go home to rest.

We are fearfully and wonderfully made. Our bodies are designed to tell us what is going on inside of us emotionally. I have noticed this in my own body, but now I can see it at work among my sheep.

We can see where this happened in the story of Mary and Martha, when Jesus came to their house for a visit in Luke 10:38–42. These women would normally both fly into action, providing hospitality for Him and His twelve disciples, but this time Mary decided to sit down to hear what Jesus had to say:

Now it happened as they went that He entered a certain village; and a certain woman named Martha welcomed Him into her house. And she had a sister called Mary, who also sat at Jesus' feet and heard His word. (Luke 10:38–39)

Luke noted, in his account of the story, that Martha had become perturbed enough to approach Jesus, asking, *"Lord, do You not care that my sister has left me to serve alone? Therefore tell her to help me"* (v. 40).

Telling Mary to help would have been a simple solution, but it would not have resolved the greater issue behind Martha's frustration. Jesus ministered to her by saying,

*Martha, Martha, you are **worried and troubled** about many things. But one thing is needed, and Mary has chosen that good part, which will not be taken away from her.* (Luke 10:41–42)

Martha had put herself under a lot of stress, which caused her to become frustrated with Mary and caused her to doubt that Jesus cared about her.

LOOKING BELOW THE SURFACE FOR THE SOURCES OF STRESS

Martha was caught trying to transfer her troubles to others, which is something we often do. We will try to find someone or something to blame for how we feel inside. This is the same thing David's men did when they returned and found that their city, Ziklag, had been burned and their families stolen. They wanted to kill David, yet he had done nothing wrong. He had lost his family as well, but you *gotta* blame somebody, right? This is called *transferring your stress*.

Luke was a trained medical doctor. He wrote this account many years later, likely after interviewing Mary and Martha, and felt that these details were important to the story. He noted that Jesus had perceived that the source of Martha's stress was her becoming distracted. This is an amazing insight, especially for us who often become so focused on ministry that we can miss Jesus even though He is right in our midst. He also saw worry at work under the emotions. Jesus used the words ***troubled*** *about many things* to pinpoint what was happening to her under the surface. He used the Greek word *turbid*, here, which means *to crowd*. Her being troubled clouded her judgment, making her judgmental of both Mary and Jesus.

Think back to the last time you came home and "kicked the cat" or became *perturbed* over something so small it would normally not bother you, but it caused you to become angry at someone you love. Your being angry is not the real issue; it is what is lying below the surface that needs to be dealt with. What were you stewing about on the way home? What are you worried about? What are you afraid of? Deal with these things, and the anger will take care of itself.

Here are some common sources of stress that lurk just below the surface of our lives:

- Worry or being urgency-driven
- Being afraid or fearful
- Suppressed anger
- Becoming overcommitted
- Broken relationships
- Marriage or caring for a family
- Singleness or the stress of not having someone to share life with
- Money, either the lack of it or the abundance of it Clutter
- The pressure of having to make a decision
- The pressure of having made a bad decision and dealing with the fallout
- Health concerns

We can even be stressed about stress.

SUPPRESSED ANGER

My wife, Heather, once experienced a battle with pain that was unlike anything she had ever dealt with before. The pain was tremendous—so much so, she could not sleep or comfort- ably lay down or sit. The only relief she could find was when she was standing, but she couldn't do that all the time. She went to a doctor but was only prescribed pain relief, not a solution for the pain. She was given some of the highest doses of pain medicine that she had ever taken, but this brought no relief. She went to a chiropractor and underwent many painful treatments. None of them helped. This caused both us and the chiropractor to be perplexed.

The chiropractor sent her back to her medical doctor, who ordered an MRI, and an appointment with a neurologist. No real answers or solutions to the problem were found.

After nine months of not getting any better, my wife was depressed and in the worst condition I had ever seen her. I went to the church to pray for her. I stood in the church library asking the Lord for a solution. I told Him that I was there as her head, asking Him to speak to me and to give me a solution on my wife's behalf. No sooner had I prayed this, then I felt led to reach out for a book on the shelf in front of me. I was there to pray, not to read, but felt strangely compelled to do this. I had never seen this book before, but on the front cover it said, *Healing Back Pain*. On the back cover, it said, "If you have back pain, you can have relief without an operation, medication, or exercises."[1]

This was the moment when I found Dr. John E. Sarno's amazing book. I had been in that library many times before but had never seen this book. In fact, it was the only book in the entire library that had anything to do with back pain or sciatica.

I was astonished at how quickly the Lord had answered my prayer, so I took the book home and told my wife that I had found her solution. I also told her that I didn't think her problem was physical but that it was emotional, somehow. I could see in her pain-filled eyes that this suggestion disappointed her. She was not as excited as I was about the book, but I felt it held the hope that we were looking for. She did read it but said that she could not make any connection between her sciatica and anything emotional that had been going on in her life at that time.

Soon after this, we held our annual Camp Meeting with Sergio Canales as the main speaker. Sergio is a Chilean prophet who lives in Spain. During one of the evening services, he proclaimed, "There is someone here tonight who has pain going down your leg. You have been to the doctors, and they have not been able to help you. You have taken the medicine, but it does not help. This is because your problem is not physical; it is spiritual. If you are here tonight, stand up."

My wife stood up that night, acknowledging her need. She was prayed for, but surprisingly, the pain did not go away.

All of this caused her to really seek the Lord, asking Him what was going on. Even though God was speaking to her, it was difficult for her to accept that she could have brought this on herself. She had trouble connecting the dots between what was going on in her emotions and how it was affecting her body. God was patient, and as she spent time in prayer, she began to remember a time, months earlier, when she had become really angry at someone for something they had done. At the time, she wrote them a letter expressing her disappointment for what they had done, but also extending her forgiveness. Now the Lord was showing her that she needed to go to a deeper level. She chose to forgive more completely from the heart to a degree she had not forgiven before. (She even met the individual in person and talked about the situation, to bring closure.) The pain began to subside, and within a few days, all the symptoms were gone. She was finally free from the pain.

Dr. Sarno could have made a lot more money doing operations, but he felt it was better to help people regain their physical well-being by them connecting the dots between their anger, unforgiveness, and resentment and the pain in their shoulders, joints, neck, back, and sciatica. His premise is to use the pain as a message from our bodies telling us that we are not processing these strong emotions properly.

Unforgiveness can affect us emotionally, physically, or spiritually. In can even affect us in all three areas at the same time, which is a kind of torment. This made me wonder if this wasn't what Jesus meant in His parable in Matthew 18:34 when He said that, if we do not forgive, we will be turned over to the tormentors.

1. Dr. John E. Sarno, *Healing Back Pain* (New York: Warner Books, 1991).

CHAPTER FIVE

Sources of Stress

Stress by itself is not the problem but chronic stress can be. Without a break from stress, something will break. A recent survey found that 80 percent of U.S. adults say the coronavirus pandemic is a significant source of stress in their life, and 60 percent said the number of issues America faces is overwhelming.[1] What is crazy about this is that such a high level of stress can weaken our immune systems, making us even more vulnerable to Covid and other viruses.

Here are some common sources of stress that most of us experience.

BROKEN RELATIONSHIPS

We all have relationship issues. Even if you are a good and godly person, there is no way to avoid it. Even the apostle Paul was under stress from relating to people. We know that he wrote the first letter to the Corinthians to correct the many errors among them that had been reported to him by members of Chloe's household (see 1 Corinthians 1:11). This was not well received. So, he wrote a second letter, about how much stress writing the first Epistle had caused him:

For out of much affliction and anguish of heart I wrote to you, with many tears, not that you should be grieved, but that you might know the love which I have so abundantly for you. (2 Corinthians 2:4)

Having to confront people is never easy for me. It has been the source of a lot of stress in my life. I would rather not do it at all, but if you love them, you will speak the truth where it will bring freedom. I wish there were guaranteed results, but too often people become offended, and the relationship fails. Paul was concerned about how the Corinthians would react to his directness. You can see his relief when Titus returned from a trip to Corinth with the following report:

For indeed, when we came to Macedonia, our bodies had no rest, but we were troubled on every side. Outside were conflicts, inside were fears. Nevertheless God, who comforts the downcast, comforted us by the coming of Titus, and not only by his coming, but also by the consolation with which he was comforted in you, when he told us of your earnest desire, your mourning, your zeal for me, so that I rejoiced even more. (2 Corinthians 7:5–7)

MARRIAGE

A lot of our stress comes from the marriage relationship:

But I want you to be without care. He who is unmarried cares for the things of the Lord—how he may please the Lord. But he who is married cares about the things of the world—how he may please his wife. There is a difference between a wife and a virgin. The unmarried woman cares about the things of the Lord, that she may be holy both in body and in spirit. But she who is married cares about the things of the world—how she may please her husband. And this I say for your own profit, not that I may put a leash on you, but for what is proper, and that you may serve the Lord without distraction. (1 Corinthians 7:32–35)

Stress comes from the cares of this world or endeavoring to make life work. Much of the stress within marriage arises because our flesh is often in conflict with the flesh of our spouse. Paul talked about stress being added to our already stress-filled lives.

If you think you can escape stress through divorce, think again. You are just trading one stress for another. Whenever I have walked with those going through a divorce, I am always amazed by the amount of stress the legal system puts on an already fractured relationship. It is always a shock to find that divorce does not solve anything, and if there are children involved, the spouses will always be in each other's lives.

SINGLENESS

While single people may have less stress than married people, they are not exempt from it:

I suppose therefore that this is good because of the present distress— that it is good for a man to remain as he is: Are you bound to a wife? Do not seek to be loosed. Are you loosed from a wife? Do not seek a wife. But even if you do marry, you have not sinned; and if a virgin marries, she has not sinned. Nevertheless such will have trouble in the flesh, but I would spare you. (1 Corinthians 7:26–28)

I meet a lot of young adults who are stressed out about being single. It doesn't help matters much either when people treat their singleness as if there was something wrong with it, or that all their problems will go away if they only find someone to marry. Here is what Paul thought of this, as seen in the *Message* translation:

Are you married? Stay married. Are you unmarried? Don't get married. But there's certainly no sin in getting married, whether you're a virgin or not. All I am saying is that when you marry, you take on additional stress in an already stressful time, and I want to spare you if possible. (1 Corinthians 7:26–28)

KIDS

Having kids creates its own stress because it is such a great responsibility. If they are not properly trained, it can add stress to our stress. I have written a little booklet based upon the premise that our kids have a fallen nature that comes from Adam. It needs to be controlled, but until they can learn to yield to the Spirit for self-control, they need our help controlling it. Most of what they do is a result of our training, whether it is good training or bad, and the Bible says that they will not depart from it (Proverbs 22:6). We can train them to obey only after we become angry, or we can train them to respond the first time we calmly tell them what we want them to do. It is all in the training, which can result in our hearts and homes becoming less stressful.[2]

MONEY

Not having enough money can create stress, but having more of it is rarely the solution God applies to relieve stress. Usually, there needs to be a change of perspective and a change in how to do life. You would think having more money would solve your problems and reduce stress, but this is rarely the case. In fact, Jesus talked about the stress that comes with having too much wealth (see Matthew 6:19–21). It causes people to lose sleep and their spiritual priorities, and even lose their souls.

John D. Rockefeller's life was almost ruined by his great wealth. A billionaire at the age of fifty-three, Rockefeller was earning about a million dollars a week but was too sick to enjoy any of it. He was confined to his bed, unable to sleep, existing on a diet of milk and crackers because of worry. When he started giving his money away, his health improved, and he went on to celebrate his ninety-eighth birthday.[3]

CLUTTER

The accumulation of things often creates stress for us. You must maintain, store, manage, and keep safe all the stuff you have acquired. Someone once observed, "The more things you have, the less there is of you." It is amazing how decluttering our lives can reduce stress. One rule of thumb is that if you did not need it during the past year, you may not need it at all. The more you have, the less there is of you!

BAD DECISIONS

At the same time, you need to "own" anything that you feel convicted about. If God shows you that you have done some- thing to bring your troubles upon yourself, own it right away. Don't blame others or circumstances. The more forthright you are, the quicker you can move forward. I found a Bible verse that I paraphrased that has helped me do this:

> *You brought this problem on yourself, but in Me is your help.* (Hosea 13:9–10)

Begin by making a list of the things that cause stress in your life (use napkins if need be), and then make a list of the physical symptoms you are experiencing. Finally, make a list of ways you will try to learn to relax in order to recharge.

OUR FLOWERS ARE FADING

A surprising source of stress mentioned in the Bible is the process of growing older. I find it interesting that both the apostles James and Peter took time to write about how our lives are like flowers and grass:

> *Let the lowly brother glory in his exaltation, but the rich in his humiliation, because as a flower of the field he will pass away. For no sooner has the sun risen with a burning heat than it withers the grass; its flower falls, and its beautiful appearance perishes. So the rich man also will fade away in his pursuits.* (James 1:9–11)

> *Since you have purified your souls in obeying the truth through the Spirit in sincere love of the brethren, love one another fervently with a pure heart, having been born again, not of corruptible seed but incorruptible, through the word of God which lives and abides forever, because "All flesh is as grass, and all the glory of man as the flower of the grass. The grass withers, and its flower falls away, but the word of the Lord endures forever." Now this is the word which by the gospel was preached to you.* (1 Peter 1:22–25)

Any middle-aged person will tell you how fleeting life is. Trying to prolong it, to stave off the inevitable, only adds pressure to our lives. Ask anyone who was once considered handsome or beautiful about the pressure they feel trying to avoid the change that comes with aging, and they will tell you that it is a constant source of stress. The Bible compares our lives to that of a flower. First, before there is even a bud on a stem, much development is occurring, but then the bud begins to blossom, and there is a short period of full bloom. No matter how beautiful or perfect the flower is, it begins to fade.

This process not only applies to beauty but can also apply to success. Ask any musician or actor about how fleeting success is. For that matter, the process can also be applied to ministries. Ask any popular preacher who once "packed them in," and they will tell you how it fades. The rise to usefulness is often looked back upon as the best part of the process. Then once they have fully blossomed, that moment does not last long. Just like a flower, their fading is inevitable.

Job is supposed to have been the first book of the Bible to be written. If that is true, then we can see how this perspective has been with us from the beginning of time:

He comes forth like a flower and fades away; he flees like a shadow and does not continue. (Job 14:2)

We don't hear much about this perspective today, but it was included in these powerful end-time Epistles as well. These days, there is not only a lot of pressure upon us to attain greatness or success, but also to keep it. Let's not put Botox into our pulpit ministries or give our image a facelift; nothing can stop a flower from fading once its time has come. It is better to age gracefully, focusing our time on helping younger folks navigate it all. Is there relief in just embracing aging as a fact of life? I think so. Understanding everyone ages or grows older can also help us cope as we go through all the changes ourselves.

The apostle Peter seemed to have been quoting the prophet Isaiah, who proclaimed:

The voice said, "Cry out!" And he said, "What shall I cry?" "All flesh is grass, and all its loveliness is like the flower of the field. The grass withers, the flower fades, because the breath of the Lord blows upon it; surely the people are grass. The grass withers, the flower fades, but the word of our God stands forever." (Isaiah 40:6–8)

In other words, if you want your life or ministry to remain relevant and your true beauty preserved, center them upon the Word of God. The Word is the only thing that lasts.

If you want to reduce your stress about fading, don't put all your emphasis on your outward appearance but focus on inner beauty, which comes from a life of love, good works, and hospitality. If you want to reduce stress about your success, put all your energy into family, friendships, giving, and serving others. Begin helping the next generation become successful and teach them how to survive it all. Being others- centered can reduce your stress by focusing on meeting someone else's need. James directed his congregation to do just that when he wrote:

Pure and undefiled religion before God and the Father is this: to visit orphans and widows in their trouble, and to keep oneself unspotted from the world. (James 1:27)

What does it profit, my brethren, if someone says he has faith but does not have works? Can faith save him? If a brother or sister is naked and destitute of daily food, and one of you says to them, "Depart in peace, be warmed and filled," but you do not give them the things which are needed for the body, what does it profit? Thus also faith by itself, if it does not have works, is dead. (James 2:14–17)

Brethren, if anyone among you wanders from the truth, and someone turns him back, let him know that he who turns a sinner from the error of his way will save a soul from death and cover a multitude of sins. (James 5:19–20)

Perhaps there is a way to evaluate yourself by creating a chart from the list of sources of stress itemized in this chapter. You could check how many of the symptoms you have, rating them on a scale from one to ten, with one being low and ten being high.

It might be helpful to read my books on learning to rest and how to get your spiritual life back through retreating. I have written a couple along this line that you can explore. (See "Addendum One: My Book List" for my recommendations.)

1. Taken from my book on child training entitled *Hand in the Cookie Jar* by Penn Clark. Here is the web address for the quotation: https://www.usatoday.com/story/life/health-wellness/2021/02/01/physical- symptoms-stress-warning-sign-mental-health-issues/4307318001/

2. David Jeremiah, *Searching for Heaven on Earth* (Nashville: Thomas Nelson Inc., 2004) p. 128.

3. Steve Brown, "Forgiven and Forgotten," *Preaching Today*, Tape No. 139.

the Lord's Prayer

No doubt the most familiar prayer in all the world is the prayer of Jesus, called the *Lord's Prayer*, which most of us learned from the King James Version of the Bible:

After this manner therefore pray ye: Our Father which art in heaven, hallowed be thy name. Thy kingdom come, thy will be done in earth, as it is in heaven. Give us this day our daily bread. And forgive us our debts, as we forgive our debtors. And lead us not into temptation, but deliver us from evil: for thine is the kingdom, and the power, and the glory, for ever. Amen. For if ye forgive men their trespasses, your heavenly Father will also forgive you: But if ye forgive not men their trespasses, neither will your Father forgive your trespasses. (Matthew 6:9–15, KJV)

I don't believe Jesus ever intended for us to simply recite this prayer in its entirety or to pray it by rote. Otherwise, it would contradict what He had just said in the previous verses:

Don't recite the same prayer over and over as the heathen do, who think prayers are answered only by repeating them again and again. Remember, your

Father knows exactly what you need even before you ask him! (Matthew 6:7–8, TLB)

What I do believe is that Jesus was giving us an outline for our own prayers, which included:

- *Our Father*: Begin by seeing God as our heavenly Father. Sometimes, I will call out to Him like a lost child calls for his Father. Many times, this is as far as I get before being overwhelmed with His glory.

- *Which art in heaven*: It helps to lift our eyes from ourselves and our circumstances to heaven. When I do this, I feel as though I am entering another realm. In fact, I am.

- *Hallowed be thy name*: I begin by worshipping Him. Worship is what "hallowing" His name means. I take time to worship Him, making up songs about Him and singing them aloud. I can never do this without feeling the Lord drawing near.

- *Thy kingdom come*: In all these years, I have never once prayed for the world to end and Jesus to come back. Instead, I think of this as inviting Him as the mighty King to come into my circumstances, my conflicts, and my struggles—to be the One in control. The thought of Him being in control of what I cannot control brings much peace to my mind.

- *Thy will be done in earth, as it is in heaven*: It is here that I come into a deeper level of surrender, yielding my will to His, wanting what He wants more than what I want. I believe He has a plan for everything, a better way of doing everything, and all I need to do is ask that it will take place. This brings heaven to earth. I do this because I believe He wrote His pleasure for my life before I even existed. I only need to surrender to His pleasure, and I begin to feel His peace.

- *Give us this day our daily bread*: While I have never once asked for bread, I have come to rely on His provision for everything. Praying this way also helps me to become more one-day minded, not borrowing trouble from tomorrow.

- *And forgive us our debts*: I do ask and receive His forgiveness so that no sin has a chance to accumulate or take root. Carrying past sins can be a serious source of stress and can hurt us physically (see Psalm 32).

- *As we forgive our debtors*: I use this as a reminder that I must extend forgiveness to others as freely as He has forgiven me. Otherwise, I may not be forgiven at all.

- *And lead us not into temptation, but deliver us from evil*: I ask for His leading in the war I am in and for His spiritual protection. I often struggle and need His grace to overcome.

- *For thine is the kingdom*: Again, I need to be mindful that He is the One in charge, the King who is in control.

- *And the power*: I need to rely upon His miraculous power to be at work in my life.

- *And the glory . . . forever*: I want to do everything for His glory and honor, both now and forever.

- *Amen*: this means so be it—let it happen, Lord!

Using this as a prayer outline, rather than a prayer in itself, is one of the best stress reducers I have found. It is difficult to remain stressed when I come to Him in worship, seeing Him as a caring, loving Father, who is ready to hear me and who wants to be involved in my daily life. It is difficult to remain stressed while seeing Him as a mighty King, surrendering to His will, trusting Him for my day-to-day provision. It is difficult to remain stressed while trusting the Father to lead me and provide spiritual protection and while looking to Him to be the source from whom I receive forgive- ness as well as offer forgiveness to those who hurt and offend me. It is difficult to remain stressed while relying on His miraculous power, doing everything for His glory, and truly expecting that what I have prayed for will actually happen.

Here is the same prayer as found in the *Message*, which contains a few more insights:

The world is full of so-called prayer warriors who are prayer- ignorant. They're full of formulas and programs and advice, peddling techniques for getting what you want from God. Don't fall for that nonsense. This is your Father you are dealing with, and he knows better than you what you need. With a God like this loving you, you can pray very simply. Like this:

Our Father in heaven, Reveal who you are. Set the world right; Do what's best— as above, so below. Keep us alive with three square meals.

Keep us forgiven with you and forgiving others. Keep us safe from ourselves and the Devil. You're in charge!

You can do anything you want!

You're ablaze in beauty!

Yes. Yes. Yes. (Matthew 6:7–13)

In prayer there is a connection between what God does and what you do. You can't get forgiveness from God, for instance, without also forgiving others. If you refuse to do your part, you cut yourself off from God's part.

TAKING TIME TO PRAY BEFORE GOING TO BED

Praying before bedtime is a good way to offload what you have picked up during the day. Praying before I sleep helps me to review what I did and what I said and then to ask for forgiveness for what I did wrong as well as to forgive those who did things that bothered me. I need to turn my heart toward the Lord in the evening, trusting Him for what lies ahead.

One woman who began to trust the Lord in this way said she knew it was working just by looking at her bed in the morning. She said, "Before, when I got out of my bed, it was all rumpled because I had tossed and turned all night. Now when I get out of the bed, it's as smooth as silk."[1]

CASTING YOUR CARES

Peter gave the same advice as Jesus did, only Peter described it in terms of care. The more responsibility we carry, the more care we tend to carry. Irresponsible people don't usually suffer much from worry. I often can spot those who the super- responsible people just by their stress level.

The apostle Peter was writing to the pastors of the churches that he was responsible for, as he closed his letter with some words of advice, he warned them of things that could hurt them. Among the list of things that the apostle shared with the other leaders was a line so small that you could read right over it, but it contained a giant truth:

> *Casting all your care upon Him, for He cares for you.*
> (1 Peter 5:7)

Here is the same verse in a variety of translations, which sheds more light on what Peter was saying:

> *Casting the whole of your care [all your anxieties, all your worries, all your concerns, once and for all] on Him, for He cares for you affectionately and cares about you watchfully.* (AMP)

> *You can throw the whole weight of your anxieties upon him, for you are his personal concern.* (JBP)

> *Let him have all your worries and cares, for he is always thinking about you and watching everything that concerns you.* (TLB)

> *Live carefree before God; he is most careful with you.* (MSG)

The *rolling* part is the best part. Rolling involves giving the responsibility to the Lord. By making Him responsible, we don't have to carry the weight of the responsibility any longer. When the Lord is responsible, He does not let it fall between the cracks or rot on the shelf. He looks after it as if it were His responsibility. Rolling it upon the Lord is actually what it means when Peter wrote to the pastors in 1 Peter 5:7, telling them to *"cast your care upon the Lord, for He cares for you."* The word *casting* here involves rolling it upon the Lord. The word *care* in this verse has to do with responsibility. We could say, "Roll your responsibility upon the Lord for He is responsible for you."

This is best illustrated in Abraham taking Isaac up the mountain to sacrifice him to the Lord in Genesis 22:8. As Abraham and Isaac made their journey, carrying the wood, knife, and coals, Isaac asked his father where the lamb was. Abraham, knowing that he had been asked to offer his promised son, said, "My son, God will provide for Himself the lamb for a burnt offering" (v. 14). In the Hebrew, the term *God will provide* was *Jehovah-Jireh*, which is what Abraham named that place. (I have always paraphrased *Jehovah-Jireh* as *"God will see to it."*)

When we give our worries to the Lord, we are asking Him to "see to it." When our worries try to come back again, we simply say, *"God will see to it."* We will find that He is very a responsible Person, who looks after whatever we put in His big hand.

---

1. Adapted from my book *Come Aside* (Penn Yan, NY: Wordsmith Publishing, 2017).

CHAPTER SEVEN

One-Day Thinking

Jesus, more than anyone else, mastered what I call *one-day thinking.* That is, He lived in the moment. His schedule was not so booked up that He couldn't change it as needed or accept a spontaneous invitation to lunch (see John 4:40). As He went from town to town, He obviously traveled light. He didn't accumulate things in anticipation that something might go wrong. He left no footprint. When He died, all He left behind was the clothes on His back. He didn't just look to God for His own needs, but He made sure those around Him were taken care of. You can see one-day thinking at work by the way He got up in the morning and took His breakfast right off the tree (see Matthew 21:18–19).

The way Jesus chose to live becomes even more apparent by what He taught His disciples. He told them not to worry about the future, but to take each day as it came:

- Be in the moment. *So don't be anxious about tomorrow. God will take care of your tomorrow, too. Live one day at a time.* (Matthew 6:34, TLB)

- Only think in terms of daily bread. *Give us our food again today, as usual.* (Matthew 6:11, TLB) More than a day's worth tends to become wormy and stink. Just think of the manna from Moses' day (see Exodus 16:19–21).

- Don't think too far ahead. *But when they arrest you and deliver you up, do not worry beforehand, or premeditate what you will speak. But whatever is given you in that hour, speak that; for it is not you who speak, but the Holy Spirit.* (Mark 13:11)

- Don't carry two coats, anticipating a need or safeguarding against it. *And He said to them, "Take nothing for the journey, neither staffs nor bag nor bread nor money; and do not have two tunics apiece."* (Luke 9:3)

Applying these to our lives will help us enter into one-day thinking, which is the most freeing way to live.

By now, you might be asking, "Do you live this way, Penn?"

No, but it is something I am aware of and something I have used as a guide for many years. I don't always get it right, but at least I have a point to come back to.

"Is it practical in today's world?" you might ask.

No, but if you are reminded of it from time to time you can begin to offload things you don't need and strive for simplicity.

PAUL'S ADVICE

The apostle Paul tapped into one-day thinking. He also traveled light, leaving nothing behind, except what he wrote to others:

> *Not that I have already attained, or am already perfected; but I press on, that I may lay hold of that for which Christ Jesus has also laid hold of me. Brethren, I do not count myself to have apprehended; but one thing I do, forgetting those things which are behind and reaching forward to those things which are ahead, I press toward the goal for the prize of the upward call of God in Christ Jesus.* (Philippians 3:12–14)

Anyone who has been a recovering addict will tell you that you can only stay free one day at a time. I have worked with people trying to get free, and they always are reduced to doing only what can be done today. There is always grace just for today. They have to let go of the past and not venture into the future, taking it one day at a time. When they do this, they often find that:

- there is strength for today.
- there is always grace for today.
- personal revival is available for today.
- their marriages are only as good as they are today.

The concept of one-day thinking not only applies to our physical needs, but our emotional ones as well. Paul chose to become unburdened from his past. Philippians 3:13, more than any other, gives us permission to live in the moment, letting go of our past regrets and mistakes, the things that brought us shame, and allows us to become more forward thinking.

JUST FOR TODAY

I found a list of things called *Just For Today*. The author wrote things like, "Just for today I choose to be happy." Abraham Lincoln once said that *"most folks are about as happy as they make up their minds to be."* My happiness does not depend upon my circumstances, but it depends on the choice I make—the choice to be happy.

The list in *Just For Today* was helpful. The list went on at length, but not all the items on it spoke to me. I liked the basic idea enough that I decided to write my own list. You can do the same:

- Just for today, I will choose to meditate upon good things. I will take control of my thoughts and feelings, not the other way around.

- Just for today, I will learn something new and useful from God's Word. I will read a portion of it that requires effort, thought, and concentration. This will stretch me.

- Just for today, I will venture into a part of the Bible I do not normally read, just because I can.

- Just for today, I will take care of my body. I will exercise it, care for it, nourish it, not abuse it nor neglect it, so that it works the way God designed it to work.

- Just for today, I will do something good for someone, without them knowing it was me.

- Just for today, I will do at least two things that I don't want to do, just to go against my flesh.

- Just for today, I will compliment people rather than criticize them. I will not find fault with anything nor try to improve anyone to satisfy myself.

- Just for today, I will love my spouse in such a way that she feels God's crowning favor upon her head.

- Just for today, I will eliminate all hurry and indecision. I don't have to decide or do anything out of pressure.

- Just for today, I will write a short note of affirmation or encouragement to someone.

- Just for today, I will quiet my heart and mind. I will take time to relax.

- Just for today, I will take time to think about my heavenly Father, giving honor and gratitude to Him for who He is and for all He has done.

- Just for today, I choose not to be afraid of what might happen.

- Just for today, I choose to let go of past regrets and shame, resting in God's forgiveness and understanding.

- Just for today, I choose to love those who do not love me or those who are not very lovable.

- Just for today, I choose to set someone free with the authority I have been given to forgive.

- Just for today, I will try to live as though this were my last day. What would I do with it if it were?

CHAPTER EIGHT

Taking Charge of "What If"

Nobody can stop you from worrying. Your pastor can't, your spouse or parents can't, and neither can your best friend. Even Jesus won't make you stop worrying. He seemed to think that we could take charge of our own anxiety and not let it take over our lives. He said,

Let not your heart be troubled; you believe in God, believe also in Me. (John 14:1)

Peace I leave with you, My peace I give to you; not as the world gives do I give to you. Let not your heart be troubled, neither let it be afraid. (John 14:27)

In Matthew 6:25–34, we find the most extensive teaching that Jesus ever shared about one of the most common sources of stress. He not only described it, but also gave solutions to help deal with it:

Therefore I say to you, do not worry about your life, what you will eat or what you will drink; nor about your body, what you will put on. Is not life more than food and the body more than clothing? Look at the birds of the air, for they neither sow nor reap nor gather into barns; yet your heavenly Father feeds them. Are you not of more value than they? Which of you by worrying can add one cubit to his stature? So why do you worry about clothing? Consider the lilies of the field, how they grow: they neither toil nor spin; and yet I say to you that even Solomon in all his glory was not arrayed like one of these. Now if God so clothes the grass of the field, which today is, and tomorrow is thrown into the oven, will He not much more clothe you, O you of little faith? Therefore do not worry, saying, "What shall we eat?" or "What shall we drink?" or "What shall we wear?" For after all these things the Gentiles seek. For your heavenly Father knows that you need all these things. But seek first the kingdom of God and His righteousness, and all these things shall be added to you. Therefore do not worry about tomorrow, for tomorrow will worry about its own things. Sufficient for the day is its own trouble.

Here is how *Strong's* defines *worry*:

> **WORRY** GK. 3308 *merimna*; from 3307 (through the idea
> of distraction); solicitude:— care.

> **WORRY** GK. *merimnao*; Strong's GK 3309: From *merizo*, "to divide into parts."

The word *worry* suggests a distraction. When put in the context above, it means being distracted by or preoccupied with the future, how things will play out, how we will be provided for. I call these "what ifs." They always cause anxiety, stress, and pressure. Jesus wanted us to replace worry or "what if" with the assurance that we are under the watchful care of a heavenly Father, who is ever mindful of our needs.

BE ANXIOUS FOR NOTHING

The following advice was given by Paul in a letter written from prison in Rome:

Be anxious for nothing, but in everything by prayer and supplication, with thanksgiving, let your requests be made known to God; and the peace of God, which surpasses all understanding, will guard your hearts and minds through Christ Jesus. (Philippians 4:6–7)

As someone caught in the Roman prison system, Paul wanted to use what he was learning and experiencing to bring comfort to a young church going through its own pressure from persecution. He told them to replace worry with prayer, supplication, and thanksgiving, which would allow God's peace to act as a guard to their hearts.

Anxiety can put pressure on us to act, take matters into our own hands, or quit the process of prayer altogether. Anxiety also makes waiting a lot harder than it needs to be. To counter this, Paul taught the Philippians how to pray in a certain pattern.

Paul started off by saying that we must pray, then supplicate with thanksgiving. Prayer, supplication, and thanksgiving are three completely different aspects of prayer. The word *prayer* here has to do with conversational kinds of prayer, where you talk things over with the Lord, telling Him what you are thinking and allowing Him to tell you what He is thinking. This is followed by *supplication*, which means to make a petition or a request. Keeping the order of this pattern is key. As a pastor, I get to listen to a lot of people pray and have noticed how much they pray like little children. If you listen to children pray, they tend to stay with these two aspects of prayer but fail to talk things over with the Lord. They usually fail to follow this pattern that ensures peace of heart and mind. If you don't talk things over with the Lord but launch right into telling God your request, you will remain anxious. Here is a sure way to reduce anxiety and bring about peace of heart and mind:

- **Conversational prayer:** Talk things over with the Lord as if He does not know what is happening. This will do your heart a lot of good. Explain what you are thinking and feeling. Then, ask Him questions, waiting for His input.

- **Request:** Based upon His input, make your request to Him.

- **Thanksgiving:** Now stand in prayer, giving Him thanks for what He is about to do.

If anxiety tries to come back, just continue to thank the Lord for doing what He said He would do as you prayed about it. Thanksgiving will not only act like a lifejacket to keep you from drowning in a sea of despair, but it contains the kind of faith that moves the hand of God.

THINGS TO DO NOW

Most people who burn out do so because their lives are built around their work. When work goes bad, as it can sometimes, they don't have anything else to live for. Their whole lives are wrapped up in their work. There must be more to life than our work. It is better to live a diversified life.

Retire a little every day. I am not advocating a life of leisure. In fact, I think a life of leisure would be an empty life. Instead, I am saying we should live productive lives with moments of leisure built into them. It seems to me that people are postponing all the good stuff until they can fully retire. Rather than waiting to retire, retire a little every day.

- **Take a day off from your struggles.** You can choose not to think about your bills, your work, or struggles for one day a week.

- **Set aside time to relax.** Include time for guilt- free relaxation into your daily schedule. Don't allow what other people think to cramp this. It is not a selfish thing to do. This is simply time to take a break from all responsibilities and recharge your batteries so you can be at your best.

- **Spend time with positive people** whom you truly enjoy, even if it is for thirty minutes. This can act as a medicine to help take the edge off the negative aspects of stress.

- **Look forward to something you enjoy doing every day.** Plan to do something you really enjoy each day, even if it is for an hour. It can be stargazing, birdwatching, playing your instrument, or working on a craft or project around the house.

- **Go for walks.** Taking walks are a busy man's vacation. Schedule a 30-minute walk each day and see what it does for your stress level.

- **Take a second look at creation.** You cannot look at birds or flowers for long without feeling more relaxed, reflective, and awed. Most of this can be done right in your backyard or a nearby park. Take a closer look at snowflakes and see what that does for you. You cannot remain full of stress for long if you take time to gaze at stars, sit still beside a meandering meadow, or submerge yourself in a lazy river and watch it come to life. Getting to the beach during the early hours or as the sun goes down is the best. There is medicine in sunrises and sunsets, and there are no two alike. I have become an unabashed cloud watcher. I don't know why, but I love watching them and will often marvel over them. All of creation was once in the heart of God, before He spoke it into being, so there is something of His peace in all of it.

- **Make a list.** Making a list helps reduce stress. I write out what I am struggling with on paper. I often empty my head this way, making lists of everything I need to do. There are things that are in the back of my mind, things I don't want to forget, things I want to forget, things I don't have solutions for, people I need to get to, people who bother me, concerns I have, crises that are looming, questions I need answers for, and things to pray about. I have all kinds of lists. It never fails that, when I get things all out on paper, I begin to feel lighter, better, and less stressed.

• **Eat "soul" food.** There are certain foods that are not only good for you, but good for the soul. I think there is a reason we crave pastas on cold, rainy days or soups in the winter. They affect our emotions in a positive way. Notice it was only after Isaac ate the tasty venison that he began to prophesy blessings over Jacob. Somehow, he understood that good food releases good things in and through us.

• **Take a slow-motion day.** If you cannot get the time off required to really get into rest, you can at least schedule some slow-motion days. This is where you deliberately slow down, not taking on anything you don't really have to do.

• **Make less of your vacations.** When we go on vacation, we tend to expect too much from it. We cram in so much, trying to get our money's worth, that, when we get back home, we need a vacation from our vacation. Try scaling back, keeping it simple, or better yet, allow for some serendipity in your vacation and see what happens.

- **Avoid the big why questions**. Steer clear of the "why questions" as they tend to add stress to your life and postpone your being able to get through your situation. Knowing why will not add any faith to your life and rarely changes anything.

  If it is critical that you know why in order to get the victory in your situation, the Lord will let you know. Instead of asking why, ask Him "what" questions, like, "What would You have me do right now so I can recover? What should I do with my time?"

You may say that this is an impractical or even irresponsible way to live. You may not be able to do this, especially if you have a family to care for, but what if you moved more toward it, even as an ideal that you know you cannot fully obtain?

CHAPTER NINE

James Under Pressure

On book of the Bible that has proven to be helpful for anyone going through a time of tribulation is the Epistle of James. Knowing the background of this book may give you even more hope as you face trials and tribulations of your own. For the past two thousand years, people have drawn encouragement from his powerful letter, but not everyone is aware of all that James endured to write the advice he gave. He had a lot to say to the church as it had been under great pressure from a worldwide famine. He opened his letter by saying,

> *My brethren, count it all joy when you fall into various trials, knowing that the testing of your faith produces patience. But let patience have its perfect work, that you may be perfect and complete, lacking nothing. If any of you lacks wisdom, let him ask of God, who gives to all liberally and without reproach, and it will be given to him. But let him ask in faith, with no doubting, for he who doubts is like a wave of the sea driven and tossed by the wind. For let not that man suppose that he will receive anything from the Lord; he is a double- minded man, unstable in all his ways.* (James 1:2–8)

Here is the same text taken from two other translations:

My brothers and sisters, be very happy when you are tested in different ways. You know that such testing of your faith produces endurance. Endure until your testing is over. Then you will be mature and complete, and you won't need anything. (James 1:2–4, GWT)

Consider it a sheer gift, friends, when tests and challenges come at you from all sides. You know that under pressure, your faith-life is forced into the open and shows its true colors. So don't try to get out of anything prematurely. Let it do its work so you become mature and well-developed, not deficient in any way. If you don't know what you're doing, pray to the Father. He loves to help. You'll get his help, and won't be condescended to when you ask for it. Ask boldly, believingly, without a second thought. People who "worry their prayers" are like wind-whipped waves. Don't think you're going to get anything from the Master that way, adrift at sea, keeping all your options open. (James 1:2–8, MSG)

WHAT WE KNOW ABOUT JAMES

This becomes more meaningful when we hold it up to a back- drop of intense trials and severe personal pressure. First of all, can you imagine growing up with Jesus as your older brother? He was perfect, doing everything perfectly, so by contrast, it makes everything you think, do, or say, look bad. Talk about stress!

James would have been next in line to at least six siblings (see Matthew 13:55 and Mark 6:3). Then things got really weird when your oldest brother started acting like the Messiah, the Savior of the world. Not only that, but some people actually believed He was the One everyone had been waiting for. A movement began spreading everywhere, but it was always in conflict with the established religious authorities. It must have been difficult to accept that your brother was the One Moses prophesied about, the Prophet to whom everyone should listen. It was all difficult for James to believe (see John 7:5). James heard stories of his brother coming into conflict with the religious leaders of the day, going to Temple, and turning the place upside down. Then, he heard stories, incredible stories, of the miraculous things Jesus did. There was a big buzz about Him everywhere James went, especially since that day when He came back to town and told everyone that Isaiah was talking about Him. That was the day all James's family, friends, and neighbors tried to throw Jesus off the side-hill into the garbage dump.

When they heard stories that Jesus was no longer eating, the whole family went to get Him, to bring Him home, thinking He had really lost it, but that didn't go as planned (see Mark 3:21). Everyone was divided over Him, some believing He was the Messiah and others denouncing Him as a deceiver who was deceived. All of this put stress on Mom, who didn't say much, but was obviously concerned (see Luke 2:19). Then everything went wrong. James heard that Jesus had been arrested and tried as a criminal. How embarrassing! It was difficult to go out in public anymore. Jesus was supposed to be the great Savior, but ended up dying Himself, in such a painful and shameful way. James couldn't even bring himself to say the word *crucifixion*. That was just for the worst criminals. Then a few days later, everyone was saying that Jesus was alive again. James didn't know what to think or believe. All he wanted to do was to have a normal life, raise his family.

Then, there were all those rumors circulating around about Jesus' body being stolen and people actually seeing Him after He had died. James did not know what to think about all this, until the moment when Jesus, the risen Christ, stepped into his life. How gracious of Jesus to take the time to personally appear to James after He had risen from the dead (see 1 Corinthians 15:7). I think this would have been a major consolation to His younger brother, who had been put through so much, not because of anything he had done, but because of his proximity to Jesus. Perhaps the Lord did this because He understood what James had been through and the stress he was under. It had to have meant a lot to James to know that everything that had happened in his developmental years was part of God's plan, God's larger purpose, and that he was not crazy after all.

His big brother Jesus really was the Messiah. Perhaps Jesus took James through the Scriptures, like He did the men on the road to Emmaus, explaining from the Law, the Prophets, and Psalms, how the Christ had to suffer. Perhaps He explained God's plan for His coming, the way

He lived, why He had to die and be raised from the dead, according to plan.

It all made sense to James now. Besides, Mom could not have been happier. She said she had known all along but could not explain it to anyone.

A NEW CHURCH WAS BORN

When the Day of Pentecost came, the 120 followers were assembled in the upper room, including James and his siblings. He became part of the Church from the first day, and along with the rest of his family, he received the mighty baptism with the Holy Spirit (see Acts 1:14).

What joy-filled days those first ones must have been. Yet, this did not exempt James from pressure. Soon, there were thousands of baby Christians to care for. No fruit should be lost. Everyone needed teaching and encouragement during the first days of persecution which quickly followed. Like the rest of us, I am sure James must have thought that Peter was going to oversee the new church, but then, after such a short time, the apostle left the city. Next, they came to James and put the responsibility of a new, emerging, city-wide church on him. He could only have been in his late twenties or early thirties. Talk about pressure. Yet, James stayed the course and was found at the helm years later when Paul visited Jerusalem to meet with the Church leadership:

Then after three years I went up to Jerusalem to see Peter, and remained with him fifteen days. But I saw none of the other apostles except James, the Lord's brother. (Galatians 1:18–19)

Imagine the difficulty of pastoring such a sprawling church, which was measured in myriads instead of thousands (see Acts 21:17–21).

AGABUS

Soon, something happened that added pressure to the pressure. Agabus, a prophet, stood up and prophesied that there was going to be a great famine throughout all the world:

And in these days prophets came from Jerusalem to Antioch. Then one of them, named Agabus, stood up and showed by the Spirit that there was going to be a great famine throughout all the world, which also happened in the days of Claudius Caesar. Then the disciples, each according to his ability, determined to send relief to the brethren dwelling in Judea. This they also did, and sent it to the elders by the hands of Barnabas and Saul. (Acts 11:27–30)

The economy of those days was agriculturally based, so if there were no crops, there was no food, no business, no buying or selling. This meant no jobs. Not only was there nothing to take to market, but there was also nothing to eat in the markets, especially in the cities which were entirely dependent upon things coming to them from the countryside. This created a severe economic crisis. If it weren't for the new gentile churches in the small towns and in the country that had begun sending relief, the church in Jerusalem might not have survived (see Acts 11:27–30). The Jerusalem church was also grateful to the gentile churches for sending missionaries, who helped others come to know Jesus and stood with them. Relief poured in from as far away as Greece.

It is not easy pastoring people who are laid off, homebound, bored and restless.

What do you say to people who are hungry?

What do you say to people who are frustrated and angry, perhaps even at God?

What do you say to people who are dying or who have lost loved ones?

How long did all this last? Reports from this part of history vary; some say two years while others say it lasted ten years.[1] We know it was certainly more than two years because one of the first ministry trips taken by Paul and Barnabas involved bringing donations and relief from the church at Antioch of Syria to the church in Jerusalem (located some 300 miles north of Jerusalem). This occurred before the two men had taken any of their famous missionary journeys. Near the end of Paul's life, about thirty years later, he was still directing the church in Corinth about how to take their relief offering to

Jerusalem (see 2 Corinthians 8–9). No matter how long the actual famine lasted, the effect of it lasted most of Paul's adult life.

Moreover, even greater pressure arose for James. Some of the men from his church in Jerusalem had gone out among the new gentile believers, telling them that they needed to be circumcised to be saved. We can see how legalistic and intimidating this was by reading what Paul wrote of an encounter he and Peter had with these men in Galatians 1. What they were teaching was not only contrary to the gospel of grace that Jesus had given to Paul, but it almost split the entire movement. Today, we have so many denominations, but back then, there was only one Church. It could have also brought all the relief to a halt.

In Acts 15:13–21, we read that it was James who finally stood up to address the issue, making a final judgment that averted the split.

JAMES'S APPROACH TO STRESS

Now let's go back and read what James had to say about stress and trials. His advice is not something off the cuff, mere rhetoric, but something deep and heartfelt, coming from someone who understood what the Church was going through at the time:

Dear brothers, is your life full of difficulties and temptations? Then be happy, for when the way is rough, your patience has a chance to grow. So let it grow, and don't try to squirm out of your problems. For when your patience is finally in full bloom, then you will be ready for anything, strong in character, full and complete. If you want to know what God wants you to do, ask him, and he will gladly tell you, for he is always ready to give a bountiful supply of wisdom to all who ask him; he will not resent it. But when you ask him, be sure that you really expect him to tell you, for a doubtful mind will be as unsettled as a wave of the sea that is driven and tossed by the wind; and every decision you then make will be uncertain, as you turn first this way and then that. If you don't ask with faith, don't expect the Lord to give you any solid answer. (TLB)

Adversity reveals a lot about us as a people and about us as a church. What has this Covid trial revealed about you? What did it reveal about your church?

James seemed to think that approaching trials with joy would help. Trials need to be faced head-on with optimism. From this letter, James seemed to think that having good emotional endurance was the pathway to everything else we need, spiritually speaking.

Covid has raised questions like why, how long will this last, or how can we get out of this? James was more focused on these questions:

1. How can we grow spiritually?
2. How can we grow in character?
3. What can we do to become more mature?

James also felt that having wisdom was key. Wisdom is usually future tense. It involves being able to perceive what is coming so we can know how to respond. It is not about being smart as much as having the right response to whatever comes our way, either positive or negative. David became famous in his day for having this kind of wisdom. People marveled that such a young man knew how to behave himself. I believe David tapped into this by worshipping God under all kinds of circumstances, especially in adversity.

Another aspect of wisdom that is key is *perspective*. There are times when perspective is everything. Perspective is a particular way of looking at things. As believers, perspective helps us see ourselves or our circumstances through God's eyes. It only comes when we ask God for it, and His outlook comes whenever we worship, not when we are angry or upset.

Jesus did not shield those who first followed Him from emotional hardship. Neither did He shield James and His earthly family from pain or stress. Nor will He shield us from trials today but will give us perspective while we are going through them.

What James wrote has brought comfort and encouragement to many through the years. It is the go-to section of the Bible for those who have suffered bewildering loss. In light of this, read it again, knowing it comes from a young man forged in great trials from his youth upward—from a young man who found a way to grow in spite of it.

Here is what James said about stress and how to equalize the pressure:

- First, it is a trial, which means that our faith is being tested (James 1:2).

- The way to equalize the pressure is to count whatever happens as an opportunity to rejoice, counting it all joy. You will find that worshipping God in the midst of it becomes essential to your getting through it.

- In a trial, you find out what really matters in life. After everything is stripped away, you find out what is really important, as it is all you have to hold on to (v. 3).

- A trial is a test of faith, which requires endurance. If you simply stay with it, you will eventually find out that you are more complete than before and lack nothing essential (v. 4).

- In a trial, having wisdom is everything. You need to see things from God's perspective (v. 5).

- You need to hear from Him, in the midst of all the confusion that is blowing everyone else away (v. 6).

- You hear best when you remain positive and prayerful, worshipping the Father. It is like putting your antenna up. Being negative or critical causes it to retract.

- You find out that you can trust Him through it all, even though you won't have all the answers at once.

I have found one thing that's sure to block our ability to receive what we need from God. It is when we become tense, put stress upon ourselves, or become anxious. Tension, stress, and anxiety are always counterproductive. When James said to count trials pure joy, which often feels counterintuitive, it puts us in the best posture to receive whatever we need from God. Otherwise, we will be acting like a double-minded man, hesitant and doubting, unable to receive what we need.

James wrote this as if there were a sequence to it.

- First, it begins with keeping your joy, remaining optimistic, which helps you endure.

- Being able to endure emotionally leads to growth and mature responses.

- Ask Him for wisdom—expecting Him to give you a different outlook.

- Gaining God's perspective is everything.

- You will begin to see everything through His eyes.

- It is not just getting through the trial, but we need to grow in it.

Counting it all joy does not mean that you need to be happy about everything. It means being calm, cheerful, keeping your joy (*chara* GK. 5479). Someone once said, "I wouldn't trade my joy for all the happiness in the world."

---

1. Reports from this part of history vary; some say two years while others say it lasted ten years. Josephus, the Jewish historian, supplies further information concerning the intensity of this famine, with its great distress and many deaths. In a footnote, it is indicated that it may have lasted for a three-year period.

The fourth century historian Orosius mentions this famine in Syria which occurred in AD 46 and 47.

During the reign of Claudius, several different famines are known to have occurred. The first famine during this period was centered around the city of Rome in the years AD 41 and 42.

The second famine known to have occurred during the reign of Claudius was in the fourth year of his office (AD 45), and was particularly centered in Judea. It is this famine to which Luke refers in Acts 11:28.

The third famine during the time of Claudius was centered in Greece in about AD 50. The fourth famine took place in AD 52 and, once again, plagued the city of Rome. This makes the famine worldwide in scope.

CHAPTER TEN

Gaining a Heavenly Perspective

During the early days of Covid, I was surprised by how often the Lord would wake me up, giving me messages in the night. Sometimes, they were just starter thoughts that became sermons, and other times, they were complete sermons, none of which I had ever preached before. He gave me a fresh perspective, which not only helped me navigate that crazy time, but brought peace and security to our church. We not only grew during the next year, but thrived, due in part to the perspective we gained in those early days.

I am not an "end times" kind of guy, preaching about tribulation and trials, but I was getting this kind of message during Covid. I have a few books along this line in my library, but only because people have given them to me. It just wasn't within my interest, but now it was clearly coming into view. In light of this, let's see what the apostle John had to say about tribulation and the perspective we need while going through it.

I have been to the Island of Patmos before, taking an early morning boat from a port in Turkey, with the sun rising before me. It is not a large island, but bigger than I thought it would be. I learned that it is home to about 400 churches, which are more like private chapels, visited by Greek Orthodox priests, on a pay-for-prayer basis. Once we landed, we made our way to the top to the grotto where John was supposed to have received his revelation. What I liked best was the view. There is something about seeing all the white houses standing in contrast to the bluest blue Aegean Sea.

This was the island where the apostle John had lived in isolation, "quarantined" as it were, by the government, so he could no longer infect the people of Ephesus with his presence and message. Little did they know what the Lord had in store for the aged apostle, who would not only see an increase in influence, but would gain perspective like he never had before. He would not only see the churches over which he had been given oversight, but would be shown the future for all churches and the ever-increasing tribulation that was to come.

It started off like any other Lord's day for John; he arose early and found a familiar place to pray. He knelt down and began to worship. Little did he know that this act would lead to a revelation containing great hope and comfort, a fresh calling for him, and a glimpse of the future for all mankind.

First, John was given a revelation of Jesus. He had seen Him at age thirty, out in the wilderness where John was baptizing. The young disciple was likely present when Jesus came out of the water, freshly baptized with the Holy Spirit. He would have seen Him sitting around countless campfires, night after night for the next three and a half years. He had seen his dust-covered form walking endless roads all over Israel, and even walking on water a couple of times. John saw Jesus transfigured on the mountain, radiant as light itself, as Jesus talked with Moses and Elijah about the kind of death He would soon endure. John had seen Jesus being arrested, spit upon, mocked, crucified, and then walking through thick stone walls into a locked upper room. John saw Jesus on and off over the next forty days, as Jesus taught the disciples about the Kingdom. John was there when Jesus ascended into heaven, watching the soles of His sandals lift out of sight. Now John saw Him with feet like polished brass, with hair white as wool, eyes ablaze, and a sword coming out of His mouth. This was unlike any revelation of Jesus John had ever seen before.

Then, Jesus called John to, *"Come up here!"* causing John to ascend above the island, into heaven, where he was told to write down everything he heard and saw (Revelation 4:1). This new perspective was not given for John's comfort alone, but for all Christians everywhere, for all time.

John was given a split-screen view of what was going on in heaven and what was going on in the earth at the same time. He saw the peace of heaven and the panic on Earth. He saw the busyness of angels, the wonder of worshipping elders who once lived on the earth and the splendor of seraphim while, at the same time, he could the see the chaos on Earth, the efforts of an unholy trinity—of a beast, a false prophet, and the antichrist—bringing confusion and corruption to the people on Earth. John saw the ruthless rule of their totalitarian government, held in contrast to the all- knowing benevolent rule of the One who sat upon the throne, whose every action equaled salvation for those who received it as such. Jesus was clearly in control, nothing was happening that caught Him off guard or surprised Him. Jesus was the author of history as it played out, showing how the world began and how it would come to an end. John could not help but note the contrasts—the beauty and order of heaven and the destruction of the earth and the splendor of the New Jerusalem, standing out like a jewel against the velvety darkness, compared with the sun-scorched earth getting ready to be consumed by fire in its final days.

John noticed how the sea that once acted like the bars of his isolated island prison, preventing him from ever leaving, were now dried up, removed forever, ceasing to be. The sunrise and sunsets that marked every day on the island were now replaced by the glory of God.

John saw great tribulation, which is just another word for pressure or stress. It had been ratcheted up, growing worse over time, until it reached a point that, if the Lord had not cut it short, no one would have survived.

For then there will be great distress, unequaled from the beginning of the world until now—and never to be equaled again. "If those days had not been cut short, no one would survive, but for the sake of the elect those days will be shortened." (Matthew 24:21–23, NIV)

A SPLIT-SCREEN VIEW OF LIFE

The apostle John was able to escape the pits of Patmos this way. It started with worship, and then Jesus invited him to *"come up hither"* (Revelation 4:1). While John experienced a literal vision, I think we can experience something similar virtually, through prayer and meditation.

What Jesus showed John was a split-screen view of life, showing him what was going on in the Church, in the earth, and above it all in heaven. He could see a simultaneous cause and effect. John could not help but notice that, while the great tribulation was going on in the earth, from bad to worse, heaven was filled with worship, praise, and peace. God was clearly in control. Nothing happened without His knowing it. This brought peace to John's heart and is intended to bring peace to ours.

A worshipful response can transport us to another realm, where we can tap into the joy and peace of heaven. The apostle Paul encouraged the churches he pastored to practice this to gain a heavenly vantage point:

If then you were raised with Christ, seek those things which are above, where Christ is, sitting at the right hand of God. Set your mind on things above, not on things on the earth. For you died, and your life is hidden with Christ in God. When Christ who is our life

appears, then you also will appear with Him in glory.
(Colossians 3:1–4)

Bear in mind that Paul wrote this bit of advice from his prison cell. He must have learned how to do this by using the power of his imagination, which is also known as biblical meditation. *The New Living Translation* renders Colossians 3:2 as *Think about the things of heaven, not the things of earth.*

I often find that I can access the peace of heaven by imagining myself walking across a sea of glass toward the One seated on the throne of grace. I know He is looking at me and listening intently. He sees and knows everything there is to know about me, which brings a peace to my heart. I also know He accepts me just as I am, not because of anything I have done. As He invites me to sit down beside Him, I share my heart with him, including all my wonderings, my cares, and concerns, as if He did not know. Doing this forces me to put into words what I am going through, which somehow brings relief from all the pressure I tend to carry. The writer of Hebrews encourages us to come before God's throne in heaven, bearing our weaknesses and struggles:

Seeing then that we have a great High Priest who has passed through the heavens, Jesus the Son of God, let us hold fast our confession. For we do not have a High Priest who cannot sympathize with our weaknesses, but was in all points tempted as we are, yet without sin. Let us therefore come boldly to the throne of grace, that we may obtain mercy and find grace to help in time of need. (Hebrews 4:14–16)

To me, setting my mind on things above means to:

- Look at life from God's perspective.

- Let go of all negative thoughts about myself, others, or my circumstances.

- Walk the "Halls of His Heart," receiving His love and affections.

As I said previously, stress is inevitable. It actually helps to see stress as a fact of life. If you viewing stress as a fault or a failure will only add more stress to your life. Realistically speaking, we will all experience some stress each day. Jesus said so. We can't avoid it altogether, but there are some things we can do to help manage it differently:

- **Get alone.** Getting alone to think and pray, to sort things out, is helpful.

- **Write it out.** Itemize everything you are carrying or caring about on a piece of paper.

- **Pray and praise.** These to things help you keep a positive disposition. Jesus said to be of good cheer. While not everything is within your control, you can choose to be of good cheer.

- **Find your peace in Him.** The only way you can keep your stress level low is by coming aside to be with Jesus, drawing your peace from Him. Personally, I enjoy camping and kayaking as ways of coming aside and receiving peace from Jesus.

- **Prevent buildup.** Don't allow stress to accumulate to the point where you live in a state of stress, which occurs when there is constant tension in your life and you finally snap.

- **Don't ignore your issues.** Deal with those unresolved issues that clutter your heart and mind, and drain away your strength.

- **Let go of your past.** This can be done through giving or receiving forgiveness, confronting people, or seeking the Lord's healing for your pains and regrets.

- **Stop living in the future**. Stop living now with the dread of what might happen. These "what ifs" are a major source of stress that rob you of your peace today.

CHAPTER ELEVEN

Ways to Decompress

In the Old Testament, people who broke the Sabbath were put to death. Today, we are not pelted with stones for not resting, but when we do not rest, we do die spiritually and often hurt our health, which can lead to a premature death.

The buildup of stress can kill our marriages as well. Experts say there are two main things that couples fight about —sex and money. These arguments often lead to divorce. I think we need to look deeper into our marital relationships to see how stress and fatigue can rob us of our desire for romance and cause us to fight over things we would otherwise not fight about. Being under stress can result in bad spending habits and poor decisions. What if the real killer of our marriages and health is simply not enough real rest?

There is an element of salvation in rest:

For thus says the Lord God, the Holy One of Israel: "In returning and rest you shall be saved; in quietness and confidence shall be your strength." But you would not. (Isaiah 30:15)

The word *saved* used here also includes the idea of being healed, protected, and preserved. Learning to rest can be our salvation for a lot of what ails us. It works like a medicine.

I've learned you cannot be exhausted and spiritual at the same time. I see many burned out Christians who continue on the treadmill, thinking they cannot afford to get off. The fact is we cannot afford to keep going like this. It hurts our health, puts a heavy strain on our families, and causes us to regress spiritually. In the end, we will be forced off.

THE VAGABONDS

Between 1915 and 1924, Henry Ford, Thomas Edison, Harvey Firestone—three leaders in American industry at the time—and naturalist John Burroughs embarked on a series of summer road trips. The idea began after Ford and Burroughs had visited Edison in Florida where they toured the Ever-glades together. Each of them expressed the need to get away from their busy schedules, the demands of the office and factories, and restore their strength through nature, good- natured comradery, and a time just for leisure. Even though they were all wealthy men, they called themselves the Vagabonds.[1]

Their trips took them from coast to coast. They roamed around a young California and into stately Maine. They enjoyed travelling the Upper Peninsula of Michigan and all through the Adirondacks in northern New York and into the Green Mountains of Vermont. They roamed the Catskills, and all the other mountains they could find in West Virginia, Tennessee, North Carolina, and Virginia.

The Vagabonds even hooked up with a couple of Presidents of the United States as they roamed, back when presidents took the summers off, both to escape the heat of Washington and the pressures of the office, as members of Congress do today.

These trips were well-organized and well-equipped. They drove Ford passenger cars and had heavy vans that carried all the household staff and equipment. By 1919, the caravan was made up of about fifty vehicles, including a kitchen camping car with a gasoline stove and built-in icebox, all designed by Henry Ford. Back then the roads were not much more than primitive paths, and motels didn't exist, so camping was the way to go. Ford also built a heavy touring car mounted on a truck chassis with compartments for tents, cots, chairs, electric lights, and a folding table large enough to seat twenty.

As I enjoyed their story by audiobook, I could not help but notice how each member of the group worked at reducing stress differently. Henry Ford would chop wood or climb trees every chance he could and loved to engage the locals to hear their stories. By contrast, Edison preferred to nap. He was quite deaf by this stage of life, so I think I get that. I personally have found that this is the fastest way to restore my own batteries, as I have lost most of my hearing. The strain of listening to catch everything everyone says can be fatiguing, not to mention the distorted background noise that keeps me on edge. I find that being alone, even if I am not sleeping, is restful both for my body and soul. I wonder if Edison discovered the same thing to be true. You would think that John Burroughs would find his rest by observing nature, but he was a complainer, who never seemed to enjoy himself or anything around him.

Eventually, because of all the publicity these "millionaire trips" generated during the Great Depression, they had to be discontinued.

The point I am making in all this is that each one of us has to find our own way to reduce stress. What works for one, may not work for another. Any suggestion I make in these notes is just that, not one sure-fire way that works for everyone.

THE WONDER OF A MIDDAY NAP

I discovered the wonder of a midday nap later in life. It was not something I liked as a young person, perhaps because I was afraid of missing out on something else. Once I had kids of my own, however, I learned how good they can be. The most difficult part was getting to the place where I could nap guilt-free. It helped to know that great men, people like President Harry Truman, took naps seriously. It's how he managed the stress of the office. He took "getting right down to the boxers" seriously. I started doing the same.

I also read somewhere that Winston Churchill's afternoon naps were non-negotiable. It was part of his daily routine. Churchill would start his day at eight in the morning by eating breakfast, answering letters, and dictating to his secretaries, all while still in bed. This burst of work was followed by a bath, then a long lunch, after which he took time to paint or play cards with his wife, Clementine. Then, it was naptime, again. Churchill would take off his clothes and climb into bed for the next two hours, reserved for solid napping. At about six-thirty in the evening, he would rise again, take another bath, and enjoy a long dinner. He finally got down to business about eleven at night because he was a night owl and a prolific writer, often working until the wee hours of the morning. Churchill felt that his naps helped him accomplish twice as much as others.

The inventor, Thomas Edison liked to boast about how hard he worked and how little he slept, usually getting only three or four hours a night. He said he would sometimes work for 72 hours at a stretch, but once when his friend Henry Ford came by the lab for a visit, Edison's assistant stopped him from going into the inventor's office because Edison was snoozing. Ford said, "But I thought Edison didn't sleep very much." To which the assistant answered, "He doesn't sleep very much at all, but he naps a lot."

Edison managed to get in a couple of three-hour naps each day. One of his associates said Edison's "genius for sleep equaled his genius for invention. He could go to sleep anywhere, anytime, on anything." Edison said he could sleep "as sound as a bug in a barrel of morphine." He would often curl up for his naps on a workbench or on the floor of his closet.[2]

THE BEST REST

While all rest is good for us, working much better than most medicines, we are so quickly offended when we are stressed out. Here are some ways I have found to decompress the pressure before we get to the place of offense.

- **Get alone in nature.** This means really being alone, to the point that you turn off your phone. This kind of aloneness happens for me when I go camping. I realize that this is not for everyone, but there is something about being outdoors in nature, simple meals over a gas stove or fire, long walks, early nights, sunsets and sunrises over water that does wonders to my stress levels. My wife's idea of camping is staying at the Holiday Inn. Either way, three days of this can restore our souls. Five days of it can reset something deeper within us. Ten days will make me a new man.

- **I try not to talk.** This is the fastest way I have found to renew my spiritual batteries. I bring along a notebook or a journal where I can empty my head of whatever has been building up within me. I call this thinking on paper. I make lists of things I am worried about, things I have to do, things I am carrying—

listing all my responsibilities and things I wonder or worry about.

- **I often ease into it.** Some people feel another kind of stress by being alone or the suddenness of going from full tilt to nothing. There are ways to ease into it, if need be, such as being with friends in the evening while keeping your days to yourself. Listening to a good book, planning one good meal out in a restaurant at some point during the day, to give you something to look forward to.

- **Try to find out who is Lord.** Some people think that it is the Lord who is "burning them out" by doing His work. I see Jesus as a master carpenter. I doubt that He misused His tools. In the same way, I cannot imagine Him ever burning us out through overuse. We are too valuable to Him. When I see people burned out and ineffective, I can only conclude that Jesus is not really Lord at that time in their lives. Something else is driving them. Jesus would not lead them into this condition, neither would He work them until they crash and burn. This does not mean we never get tired. Even Jesus got tired, but He rested so He could keep His priorities (see John 4:6).

- **I try to get under the flow of His favor again.** Often, I experience an inner rest as I draw upon God's inexhaustible supply of favor and fondness. When I lose sight of this, it creates a tension within me. Tapping into it brings about peace.

- **We need to start savoring our successes.** One of the major truths found in the book of Ecclesiastes is that savoring the fruit of your labor is a gift from God. Some people work hard to put food on the table and never really taste it. Take some time to read the book of Ecclesiastes. It will help keep things in perspective, and you will gain insight from one of the world's most successful failures.

Wouldn't it be great if we had a built-in "cruise control" so that, once we found balance for our lives, we could push a button and lock it into place? Of course, life does not work that way, and things do not stay orderly for long, so we need to find discipline for our lives—not once then lock it in, but again and again. This becomes our work. The only way I know to do this is to come aside often. I have come to see this is not only one of the best ways of rejuvenating my spiritual life, but it has also helped me find order, keep balanced, and gain perspective.

THINGS YOU CAN DO NOW

It would bring our heart some rest just to identify and cut out the things that rob us of rest each day. Here are a few suggestions:

- **Cut back on the news.** For me, a prison sentence would be having to watch a continuous news cycle that is being dumped into my living room. I may miss some things, but I keep up with the news by skimming the headlines online, without all the tension orchestrated by the media. So much of what is presented is intended to produce fear and anxiety, which leads to bigger ratings, which sells more advertising time. The media are in the business of generating stress, then offering products that are supposed to relieve it. I just don't need it.

- **Put limits on social media.** Social media can be a great tool or a great source of stress. I choose the former by limiting my time spent and what I post. I try to keep it light and informative, but don't post much of what is going on in my life on social media.

- **Stay off the roller coasters.** Decide that you are not going to get into the roller coaster of someone else's drama. Stay out of Harry and Megan's troubles. Who needs it? You don't need all the drama created on shows like *The Bachelor*. There is an old Polish saying that goes like this: "Not my circus; not my monkey." This gives you permission to pass on it. You should pass on the mountain of virtual drama that comes through our televisions, social media, and video games.

---

1. Jeff Guinn, *The Vagabonds*, Audio Book (New York: Simon & Schuster, 2019). https://www.thehenryford.org/collections-and-research/digital-resources/popular-topics/the-vagabonds/

2. Edison said he could sleep "as sound as a bug in a barrel of morphine." He would often curl up for his naps on a workbench or on the floor of his closet.

CHAPTER TWELVE

A Negativity Fast

The apostle James often talked about controlling our tongues. While he clearly stated that no man can tame the tongue, at the same time he warned the believers of his day that having an unruly tongue could be deadly (3:8). We can poison ourselves, and each other, just by the way we talk. There are times when our church will go on fasts together, and I will often include a negativity fast, where we decide not to complain or say anything cutting or critical. This helps us become more disciplined about what we say or think and reduces the stress at work in our lives.

The apostle Paul sat in a putrid prison. There, he wrote to his beloved Philippian brethren, telling them to stop complaining. He said, *"Do all things without complaining and disputing"* (Philippians 2:14). The King James Version renders this as, *"Do all things without **murmurings** and disputings."*

The word *complaining* can also be rendered as *grumbling.* If you have a tendency to grumble, do a word study about *murmuring* in the King James Version, and see what awful things happen to those who are given to grumbling. Too often, those of us who counsel people encourage them to vent, or pour out their feelings, writing out reams of things that others have done to them, not realizing that this negativity could attract even more darkness and keep them from finding positive solutions. So, this can be counterproductive.

A PRISONER OF THE LORD

It is amazing to see how a person's outlook can change every- thing. I think of Paul who wrote:

As a prisoner for the Lord, then, I urge you to live a life worthy of the calling you have received. Be completely humble and gentle; be patient, bearing with one another in love. (Ephesians 4:1–2, NIV)

Paul could have only gained this perspective from the Lord. Notice that he wasn't sitting in his cell seething with anger at the injustice of it all. Paul did not see himself as a helpless victim or a hapless pawn. He:

- wasn't a prisoner of circumstance.
- wasn't a prisoner of the Romans.
- wasn't a prisoner of the corrupt politician named Felix.
- wasn't a prisoner of the legalistic, stiff-necked Jews.
- wasn't a prisoner of the system.
- wasn't even a prisoner of the devil.

Paul saw himself being held in the hands of the One who loved him most, the One who held his future, the One in control of everything.

When we see our circumstances as being from the Lord, it can help us endure anything. We can "do the time standing on our heads," as hard-timers used to say.

If you see your own unhappiness or circumstance as someone else's fault, because they failed, then you will seethe with anger. This only attracts more darkness, which means we come under the influence of demons. You can tell by the kinds of thoughts that follow: hatred, revenge, violence, and even suicide.

I have heard some of our Chinese brethren say astonishing things like, "I had been working hard, and the Lord knew that I needed a vacation, so He put me in prison for a while."

Another persecuted brother said, "I had been asking the Lord to teach me more, so He decided to send me to His seminary; so, I went to prison for four years." This was a perspective that kept them from drowning in the darkness.

Our flesh likes to complain and is always critical. Let's deny our flesh, putting a watch over our mouths. Not only will it help us hear from the Lord more clearly, but also it causes Him to draw near. We need to be aware that the Lord is listening to whatever we are saying in our tents:

Do not grumble against one another, brothers, so that you may not be judged; behold, the Judge is standing at the door. (James 5:9, ESV)

Let's put a watch on our thoughts and our mouths and see if it does not help change our perspective. At the very least, it will impress the Judge who is standing at the door.

On the other hand, being grateful, full of thanksgiving and praise, causes evil spirits to leave us alone. We see this happening whenever David worshipped around Saul:

But the Spirit of the Lord had left Saul, and instead, the Lord had sent a tormenting spirit that filled him with depression and fear. Some of Saul's aides suggested a cure. "We'll find a good harpist to play for you whenever the tormenting spirit is bothering you," they said. "The harp music will quiet you and you'll soon be well again." (1 Samuel 16:14–16, TLB)

There is no question that praise and a positive disposition repel evil spirits. I also believe it attracts the Lord and makes us more open to His voice, presence, and perspective. I suspect that is what happened to Joseph. He came to the place where he could look past what his brethren had done to him, and he began to see that it was the Lord who sent him on ahead to save many (see Genesis 45:4–5).

Only the Lord could have given Joseph such an unusual perspective. When you are in a difficult place, perspective is everything.

ALWAYS GIVE THANKS

We should replace complaining with a habit of giving thanks. We can use thanksgiving and praise like we would a medicine, taking it at regular intervals. Get one of those pill boxes with the days of the week on it and write praise, gratitude, and thanksgiving notes and put them in each compartment and see if this does not change your perspective.

One time I had malaria and was very sick. I reminded the Lord that I loved the poor and that He said He would visit those who love the poor on their sick bed and that their health would spring forth speedily. I asked Him what it was that He wanted me to do that would help me recover. He immediately said to begin by praising Him. As I did this, a new strength filled my body. I was able to get up and get dressed and go back downstairs. There was a doctor there who gave me the medicine I needed to fully recover. By night- fall, I was well on my way to a full recovery.

LIFE AND DEATH IN THE TONGUE

I noticed in myself, and in those who are under stress, that we become prone to negative thinking, which leads to negative speaking and that can affect our emotional and physical well- being. As if we need further proof that there is an indisputable connection between what is happening within our souls and our physical health, let's consider what the Bible says about how the words of our mouths can affect what is going on in our bodies.

Solomon, the wisest man in the world, once wrote that *"Death and life are in the power of the tongue"* (Proverbs 18:21).

What if we can ruin our health by what we say? We have all met negative, sarcastic people, whose mouths are always damning people, whose health is a wreck. So often, these two things seem to go hand in glove. What if they are poisoning themselves with their own words? What if what we think and say pollutes our own spiritual lives, just as polluted surface water can contaminate a well? Solomon said as much when he wrote:

My son, give attention to my words; incline your ear to my sayings. Do not let them depart from your eyes; keep them in the midst of your heart; for they are life to those who find them, and health to all their flesh. Keep your heart with all diligence, for out of it spring the issues of life. (Proverbs 4:20–23)

The mouth of the righteous is a well of life, but violence covers the mouth of the wicked. (10:11)

He went on to pen several similar proverbs, connecting what we say to our health:

The merciful man does good for his own soul, but he who is cruel troubles his own flesh. (11:17)

A wholesome tongue is a tree of life, but perverseness in it breaks the spirit. (15:4)

Pleasant words are like a honeycomb, sweetness to the soul and health to the bones. (16:24)

A man's stomach shall be satisfied from the fruit of his mouth; from the produce of his lips he shall be filled. Death and life are in the power of the tongue, and those who love it will eat its fruit. (18:20–21)

Just as staying physically and spiritually healthy takes discipline, we will need to discipline what comes out of our hearts and mouths. You can always tell what is going on within a person by what comes out of their mouths. Our mouths tend to reveal whatever is stirring around in our hearts.

Jesus said, *"Out of the abundance of our heart our mouth speaks"* (Matthew 12:34).

A MERRY HEART

By contrast, a good disposition can be good for our health. The Bible prescribes gaining a merry heart like you would take a medicine.

A merry heart does good, like medicine, but a broken spirit dries the bones. (Proverbs 17:22)

Perhaps this explains why Jesus often told people to be of good cheer. After all, there is a relationship between the condition of the heart and the condition of the body; there is a relationship between physical and spiritual health; there is a relationship between mental attitude and physical well-being; what is going on inside the heart has a direct bearing on physical health; and what is on the inside now will eventually manifest itself on the outside.

Our attitude in the way we approach our problems and trials can actually help bring about healing. It is important to be grateful, positive, and at peace with God and man.

Here is the same verse from a couple of other translations:

A joyful heart is good medicine, but depression drains one's strength. (GWT)

A cheerful disposition is good for your health; gloom and doom leave you bone-tired. (MSG)

HOW TO GET A MERRY HEART

- **Listen to good music**. Better yet, sing to the Lord yourself. How often have you been going through a difficult time when just the right song is sung in a meeting or plays on the radio (or on a track on a CD) and it lifts your spirit?

- **Stop complaining and grumbling.** It is difficult to be grateful and complain at the same time, but we still somehow manage to do it. I think calling a moratorium on complaining is not only allowed, but needful.

- **Listen to what comes out of your mouth.** I know that some positive confession teaching has been taken to an extreme, but there is something to speaking positively. You may need to simply stop speaking negatively for a while to get on top of your feelings.

- **Step away from negative people.** You would have to leave the planet to completely get away from negative people, but you can temporarily avoid those who bring you down.

- **Become more pleasant and agreeable to be around.** You can choose to do this. Set out to edify others, and you will become edified in the process.

- **Go deep into gratitude.** You can begin by itemizing your blessings. Make a list of the things you are grateful for and take time to consider each thing on your list.

- **Keep a sense of humor.** Some of the best humor comes out of the most difficult situations.

Humor can be a very useful thing if it is kept in check. Some comedians and comedy shows need to be avoided completely because not all humor is clean and wholesome, but a good laugh is sometimes the key to a merry heart.

When we are sick, we focus on getting our bodies stronger, sometimes while neglecting to work at making our spirits stronger. What if we turned this order around? If we get the order right, it would make us well—spirit, soul, and body. Proverbs 18:14 says, *"The spirit of a man will sustain him in sickness, but who can bear a broken spirit?"*

If you are sick, get into a place where Jesus can pastor you through it, listening for His voice and being open to His perspective. He is not only a wonderful Pastor to us, but also our Physician. Remember what God said through Moses:

If you diligently heed the voice of the Lord your God and do what is right in His sight, give ear to His commandments and keep all His statutes, I will put none of the diseases on you which I have brought on the Egyptians. For I am the Lord who heals you. (Exodus 15:26)

The phrase, *"For I am the Lord who heals you,"* literally means, "I am the Lord your Physician." Invite Him to be your Doctor and do whatever He prescribes for you.

CHAPTER THIRTEEN

Learning to Breathe

Sometimes, I forget to breathe. By this I mean, I fail to remember to breathe intentionally, deeply, bringing oxygen- enriched blood to my muscles and mind. This has been wonderful in reducing stress. I notice that when I am stressed out, angry, or afraid, I hardly breathe at all. My shallow breathing limits the flow of oxygen in my blood, and my body cries out for it in a number of ways. I have heard people say, "I need space to breathe!" I get that now. Deep breathing helps me feel refreshed in body, mind, and spirit. I call this a *poor man's vacation*.

Robert Cooper, Ph.D., the co-author of *The Power of 5* talks about five-second and five-minute health tips. In it, he wrote, "Breathing from your diaphragm oxygenates your blood, which helps you relax almost instantly. Shallow chest breathing, by contrast, can cause your heart to beat faster and your muscles to tense up, exacerbating feelings of stress. To breathe deeply, begin by putting your hand on your abdomen just below the navel. Inhale slowly through your nose and watch your hand move out as your belly expands. Hold the breath for a few seconds, then exhale slowly. Repeat this several times."[1]

Often when people become afraid or angry, they start with shallow breathing, then compensate for this by breathing in more air, almost gulping it in. Neither is good for you and both can have a negative effect on your health. The goal is to do deeper, slower, and more intentional breathing. I have only recently discovered the benefits of breathing. Now I try to do it whenever I think of it, while driving, stopping at traffic lights, and whenever I feel symptoms of stress in my system.

Today we hear a lot about post-traumatic stress disorder (PTSD) which occurs when someone experiences chronic or acute stress. It is a condition that's triggered by a terrifying event—either experiencing it or witnessing it. Symptoms may include flashbacks, nightmares and severe anxiety, as well as uncontrollable thoughts about the event.

I found it interesting that veterans who have PTSD are also taught basic breathing techniques, and those who do them often do not feel the need to return for more treatment.[2]

Memory loss is part of PTSD, and it is possible that what is being called Alzheimer's today is simply a result of acute stress.

Sometimes, I am reluctant to tell people what I have discovered about breathing, for fear of being seen as a New Age nut, but it has been a blessing to me. I have run this risk of sharing it with those who have come to me with pain in their muscles and have seen it bring almost instant results. While I know this sounds crazy, one time I had a knot in the middle of my back about as big around as my fist. I began to breathe, remembering to do it at traffic lights or while waiting for something. To my surprise, it simply disappeared. I breathed that knot away!

---

1. Robert Cooper, Ph.D., the co-author of *The Power of 5* (Rodale Press, 1996), a book of five-second and five-minute health tips. Read more by going to: http://www.rd.com/health/wellness/37-stress-management-tips/#ixzz3Z24huITJ/.

2. Watch TED Talk's with Max Strom about breathing: https://www.youtube.com/watch?v=4Lb5L-VEm34) or https://www.youtube.com/watch?v=4Lb5L-VEm34&t=28s/.

ADDENDUM ONE:

My Book List

Below are books that I recommend for further reading related to stress or to living a less stressful life:

Healing Back Pain—The Mind-Body Connection by Dr. John E. Sarno

How to Stop Worrying and Start Living: Time-Tested Methods for Conquering Worry by Dale Carnegie

None of These Diseases by Dr. S. I. McMillen

God Calling by Two Listeners, edited by A. J. Russell

Healing Medicine by Derek Prince

Come Aside by Penn Clark

What Jesus Said About Keeping A Sabbath by Penn Clark

What Jesus Said About Personal Retreats by Penn Clark

The Parable of Cherry Lane by Penn Clark

ADDENDUM TWO:

Lower Back Excises

When I first went to the chiropractor, he gave me some exercises to do that would relieve me of back pain. He assured me that I could do these even while I was in pain and that they would not do any damage to my back. He gave me a sheet of paper showing me the proper way to do them, apologizing that all he had available were *Lamaze* exercises with a picture of a pregnant woman on the front. I began doing these that day and found relief right away. In fact, these have been my go-to exercises for these past forty-plus years. I do them anytime I begin to feel pain in my lower back. Often, doing them just a couple times is enough to get freedom from the pain that is starting in my lower back.

THE PELVIC PUSH

The first one he taught me was called the pelvic push.[1] He said that strengthening my abdominal and lower back muscles can effectively help prevent or decrease back pain. I tend to do these exercises slowly, trying to get all I can get out of them. I find that doing each one for 7 seconds works best for me. I try to remember to breathe deeply while doing these exercises, but I have to be intentional about it.

The simplest way to do the pelvic push is to lie down on the floor with my knees up, feet pushing firmly on the floor. I then flatten the lower part of my back against the floor, so that there is no space between my lower back and the floor. Then, I arch my lower back, while counting to 7, remembering to breathe. I do this as many times as I feel I need to stretch my back muscles.

THE CAT

The second one my chiropractor gave me is commonly known as the *cat*. I do this as an alternative to the pelvic push. I will get up on my hands and knees, while arching my back like a cat.

I will do this to the count of 7, and then I push my belly toward the floor, making my back arch the opposite direction. I will do this to the count of 7, while trying to remember to breathe. I will often alternate between this and the pelvic push.[2]

Anytime I begin to feel pain in my lower back, I get down on my knees and do the cat. Rarely do I have to do these more than two or three times before I begin to feel relief from the pain.

---

1. https://www.spine-health.com/conditions/pregnancy-and-back-pain/strengthening-exercises-back-pain-during-pregnancy/.
2. Here are links for further examples of these exercises:
https://www. lamaze.org/Giving-Birth-with-Confidence/acat/2/tag/exercise/.
https://www.dolphinmethod.com/yoga-for-pregnancy-cat-pose/.
https://www.youtube.com/watch?v=LympZqVz14s/.

— What to eat to clear out your arteries!

(Comes from Omega 6 Foods, SUGARY FOODS,)

- **Vit. K2** drives ~~cholesterol~~ the calcium into the bones.
- Foods with High **C** are good *very important*
- **Vit. E** is Good <u>very important</u> Keeps oxygen high around the heart.
- <u>Keep omega 6 very Low</u> & Keep omega ③ very high
- <u>Salmon</u> (meal) support ART. & heart muscle
- <u>Saurkraut</u> <u>very Good for you!</u> <u>Good for gut</u>, which helps heart!

over →

Sauer Kraut is loaded with Vit K2 Super food for the heart & leaking Gut

Keeps Calcium out of the arteries

ARUGULA is very good loaded with potasium & many other things

- E.V.O.O. add (the Good Kind)
- Apple cider vinegar
- Add sun flower seeds (Vit. E)
- Cheese (K2) parmessian AGed (not Kraft) no cellulos shave on your salad!
- GARLIC - Great for the heart & Blood pressure